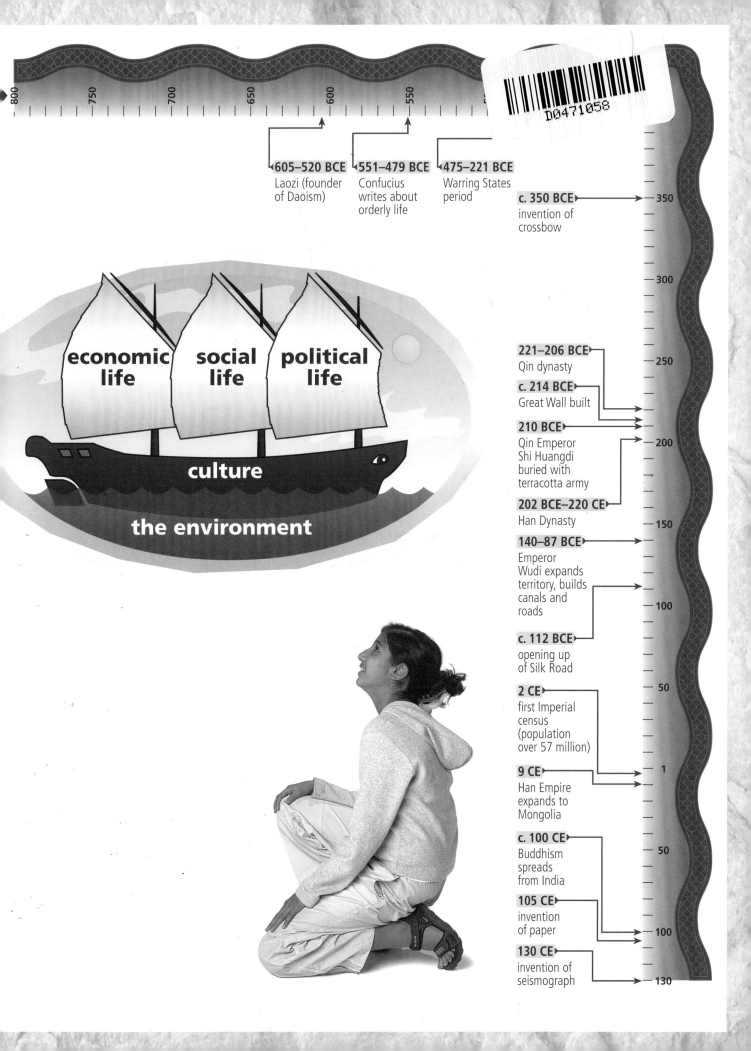

800 750 700 650 600 550

605–520 BCE
Laozi (founder of Daoism)

551–479 BCE
Confucius writes about orderly life

475–221 BCE
Warring States period

c. 350 BCE
invention of crossbow

350

300

221–206 BCE
Qin dynasty

250

c. 214 BCE
Great Wall built

210 BCE
Qin Emperor Shi Huangdi buried with terracotta army

200

202 BCE–220 CE
Han Dynasty

150

140–87 BCE
Emperor Wudi expands territory, builds canals and roads

100

c. 112 BCE
opening up of Silk Road

50

2 CE
first Imperial census (population over 57 million)

9 CE
Han Empire expands to Mongolia

1

c. 100 CE
Buddhism spreads from India

50

105 CE
invention of paper

100

130 CE
invention of seismograph

130

economic life

social life

political life

culture

the environment

D0471058

Early Civilizations

Pat Waters

DUVAL HOUSE
PUBLISHING
LES ÉDITIONS DUVAL

5 4 3

Duval House Publishing Inc.
Head Office:
18228 – 102 Avenue
Edmonton, Alberta T5S 1S7
Ph: (780) 488-1390
Tollfree: 1-800-267-6187
Fax: (780) 482-7213
Website: http://www.duvaleducation.com

Author
Pat Waters

National Library of Canada Cataloguing in Publication Data
Waters, Pat.
    Early civilizations

    Includes index.
    ISBN 1-55220-205-4

    1. Greece--Civilization--Study and teaching.
2. China--Civilization--Study and teaching.
I. Title.
DF77.W373 2001   938   C2001-911498-2

Manufacturers
Screaming Colour Inc., Friesens

Printed and bound in Canada

Validators
Educational
Olinda Brienza, Teacher
Our Lady of Grace School
Waterloo Region Catholic District School Board
Waterloo, Ontario

Dolores Cascone, Curriculum Resource Teacher
Toronto Catholic District School Board
Toronto, Ontario

Sandee Elliott, Teacher
Muirhead Elementary School
Toronto, Ontario

Historical
Dr. Jennifer W. Jay, Professor
History and Classics Department
University of Alberta
Edmonton, Alberta

Dr. Jeremy Rossiter, Professor
History and Classics Department
University of Alberta
Edmonton, Alberta

Bias Reviewer
Nora Green, Teacher
Green Glade Senior Public School
Mississauga, Ontario

Special Thanks
Danielle Stock
Waterloo, Ontario

Crestwood Urban Fare
142 Street and 96 Avenue
Edmonton, Alberta

Photographic Models
Brian Daniels   Jessica Kruhlak
Warren Ip   Salina Ladha

We acknowledge the financial support of the Government of Canada through the Book Publishing Industry Development Program (BPIDP) for our publishing activities.

Canada

Acknowledgements

The author wishes to express sincere gratitude to the many people who participated in the production of this book. I am most grateful to Karen Iversen, who put her faith in me and guided me through every detail of the process. Betty Gibbs also deserves my special thanks for her guidance as my editor and my mentor.

As well, I wish to thank many others for contributing their invaluable skills and talents to assist me in my efforts to create a worthwhile textbook for all of the children who will use it.

Many thanks to Claudia Bordeleau for creating an impressive design for this book and to Wendy Johnson for her wonderful maps. I am also indebted to Lorna Bennett, Chao Yu, and Don Hight, whose marvelous illustrations enhance the story of these ancient civilizations, and to David Strand, who sought out the numerous photographs that give authenticity to the text.

I also want to acknowledge the students involved in this production. Thanks to Brian, Salina, Jessica, and Warren, who appeared in the photographs that make this study real for students, and to my granddaughter Danielle Stock, for her wonderful story about Ikaros at the Agora. Many thanks also to my husband Ron Waters for his patience and understanding during the many phases of this project.

Project Team

Project Managers: Karen Iversen, Betty Gibbs
Editors: Betty Gibbs, Karen Iversen,
    Shauna Babiuk, Kim Doyle
Cover and Text Design: Obsidian Multimedia,
    Claudia Bordeleau
Photo Research: David Strand
Production: Claudia Bordeleau, Jeff Miles,
    Leslie Stewart
Maps: Johnson Cartographics Inc., Wendy Johnson
Illustrations: Lorna Bennett; Chao Yu; Don Hight
Photographer: New Visions Photography,
    Brad Callihoo
Photo Shoot Coordinator: Roberta Wildgoose

Picture Credits

Every effort has been made to identify and credit all sources. The publisher would appreciate notification of any omissions or errors so that they may be corrected. All images are copyright © of their respective copyright holders, as listed below. Reproduced with permission.

Legend: (t) = top (r) = right (l) = left (m) = middle
(b) = bottom
AGGV = Art Gallery of Greater Victoria, Victoria, BC

Cover: trireme - Paul Lipke/Trireme Trust; caryatid - © The British Museum; Great Wall - Keren Su/China Span **3** (mr), **114** (m), **125** (ml, mr) Science Museum/Science and Society Picture Library **5** (br), **12** (tr), **14** (tl), **65** (tl) JP Oleson **11** (ml), **45** (br), **76** (mr) CM Dixon Colour Photo Library **20** (ml, mr), **26** (mr), **29** (tr), **31** (mr), **33** (t, br), **34** (ml), **38** (mr), **50** (bl), **53** (bl), **57** (all but bl), **65** (b), **73** (mr) copyright The British Museum **26** (ml), **36**, **72**, **74** (all r) Illustrations from *Sightseers Ancient Greece* reproduced by permission of the publisher. Copyright © Kingfisher Publications Plc., 1999. All rights reserved. **86** (t), **87** (ml, bl), **88** (mr), **89** (mr, bl, br), **90** (ml, bl), **99** (bl), **100** (ml), **111**, **130** (b), **136** (ml), **139** (b), **146** (tr) Keren Su/China Span **97** (mr), **109** (ml, mr), **125** (bl), **131** (tr), **132** (bl), **145** (ml) China Foto Gallery **2** (t) © A. Woolfitt/robertharding.com (ml) © Upperhall Ltd./ robertharding.com (b) © Sonia Halliday Photographs, photo by Verity Weston **3** (t) Courtesy Greek National

Tourist Board **9** (tr) Tibor Bognár (b) Courtesy Greek National Tourist Board/M. Laloux **11** (tr) © T. Teegan/ robertharding.com (mr) G. Thouvenin/robertharding.com (bl) © J. Lightfoot/Firecrest Pictures/robertharding.com **12** (ml) © T. Teegan/robertharding.com (mr) © T. Gervis/robertharding.com **14** (bl) © 2001 PhotoDisc, Inc. **15** (tr) © D. Beatty/robertharding.com (mr) MediaFocus International, LLC (ml) © L. Wilson/robertharding.com (br) Courtesy Greek National Tourist Board/W. Tkachyk **16** (tl) Jeremy Ferguson/Spectrum Stock; (mr) © G. Thouvenin/robertharding.com (bl) © M. Busselle/ robertharding.com **19** (tr) © Dorling Kindersley (ml) Courtesy of Two-Can Publishing **22** (house) with permission of The Reader's Digest Association Limited, *Everyday Life Through the Ages* © 1992 **23** (tr) Museo Archeologico Nazionale, Naples, Italy/Roger-Viollet, Paris/Bridgeman Art Library (bl) Musée du Louvre, Paris/photo: AKG London/Erich Lessing **26** (br) Musée du Louvre, Paris/photo: AKG London/Erich Lessing **29** (tl) Musée du Louvre, Paris/photo: AKG London/Erich Lessing (bl) © Randa Bishop **32** (mr) © L. Wilson/ robertharding.com **33** (mr) Debbie Kelsey and Daniel Luebke **39** (tr) Kunsthistorisches Museum, Wien oder KHM, Wien **47** Sonia Halliday Photographs, Bibliothèque Nationale **50** (br) Kunsthistorisches Museum, Wien oder KHM, Wien **53** (t) Courtesy Greek National Tourist Board **57** (b) Private Collection/Paul Freeman/Bridgeman Art Library **59** (tl) © Sonia Halliday Photographs **60** (tr) Musée du Louvre, Paris/photo: AKG London/Erich Lessing (ml) Courtesy Greek National Tourist Board **62** (bl) Corel **64** (t) 956.118/Model of the Athenian Acropolis, with permission of the Royal Ontario Museum © ROM (mr) British Museum, London, UK/Bridgeman Art Library **65** (mr) Galleria degli Uffizi, Florence, Italy/ Bridgeman Art Library **66** (tr, mr) CODA/Olympic Hall of Fame and Museum Archives (ml) © R. Rainford/ robertharding.com (bl) reproduced with permission of the International Olympic Committee **71** (bl) Tibor Bognár **77** (tr) Paul Lipke/Trireme Trust (b) Alexandra Guest/Trireme Trust **83** (t) Tibor Bognár **86** (b) © Malie Rich-Griffith **87** (tr) © 2001 IMS Communications Ltd. www.picture-gallery.com **89** (ml) © Sonia Halliday Photographs; photo by Jane Taylor **90** (tr) © Gerald D. Tang (br) AGGV 64.172/Jade dog, Tang/Song period (8th-10th century), gift of Fred & Isabel Pollard Collection/ photo Bob Matheson **109** (bl) AGGV 92.1/Lian container, Han dynasty (206 BC-220AD), gift of Mr. and Mrs. Cheney Cowles/photo Bob Matheson **110** (tr) Oriental Bronzes Ltd., London, UK/Bridgeman Art Library **114** (b) Richard Greenhill **130** (t) © Robert Harding Picture Library/robertharding.com **131** (tl) AGGV 88.2/Tomb figure of standing woman, Han dynasty, gift of Mr. Brian McElney/photo Bob Matheson (ml) © Robert Harding Picture Library/robertharding.com (br) AGGV 91.14.45/ Earthenware censer, Han dynasty, gift of Mr. Brian McElney/photo Bob Matheson **133** (t) 923.1.30 Male Acrobat figure, Han Dynasty, mid 1st-2nd century AD, China, 923.1.23/923.1.35/922.4.16/922.4.17 Tomb figurines, entertainers and dancers. Eastern Han dynasty, mid 1st-2nd century AD. With permission of the Royal Ontario Museum © ROM **135** (ml) Private Collection/Bridgeman Art Library **136** (bl) Tim Pelling/Spectrum Stock (br) CP PHOTO/Kevin Frayer **143** (mr) © Sonia Halliday Photographs; photo by Jane Taylor **148** (tr) CODA/Olympic Hall of Fame and Museum Archives (tm) Courtesy of the Geological Survey of Canada (ml, bl, br) Corbis (mr) Corel (bm) Canadian Press/Darryl Dyck

To the Student

Our way of life today has been built on legacies from the past. Legacies are things of value that we inherit from people who are no longer living. We learn about ways that people lived in the past in order to understand our own way of life better.

Civilizations have existed throughout the world for many thousands of years. This textbook, *Early Civilizations*, will help you understand what a civilization is. It will give you a learning model for studying different civilizations. The model is applied to two examples, ancient Greece and ancient China.

The Overview at the beginning of *Early Civilizations* describes the Model for Learning about a Civilization. The organization of the book is based on the different parts of the model. This structure is used in both sections of the textbook to help you compare ancient Greece and ancient China.

Section I introduces ancient Greece. Many of the words we use in our English language came to us from ancient Greek. Our type of government, democracy, also had its origin in ancient Greece.

In Section II you will visit ancient China. The ancient Chinese people are known for their many inventions. China is also known for having the same type of government and a similar way of life for over 2000 years.

Early Civilizations provides a wealth of different sources for you to use in your learning. There are photos, illustrations, maps, charts, graphs, and stories, as well as text information. You will find a pronunciation guide, a glossary, and an index at the back of the book.

For your quick reference, there are two timelines inside the front cover of the book. They show events that occurred during the time you will be studying. These pages also display two ship diagrams that will remind you of the learning model.

You will find maps of ancient and modern Greece and China inside the back cover. These maps are also for quick reference as you study these civilizations.

Throughout the book, four Canadian children invite you to learn new skills with them and take part in many interesting activities. We hope you enjoy this journey through past times with them!

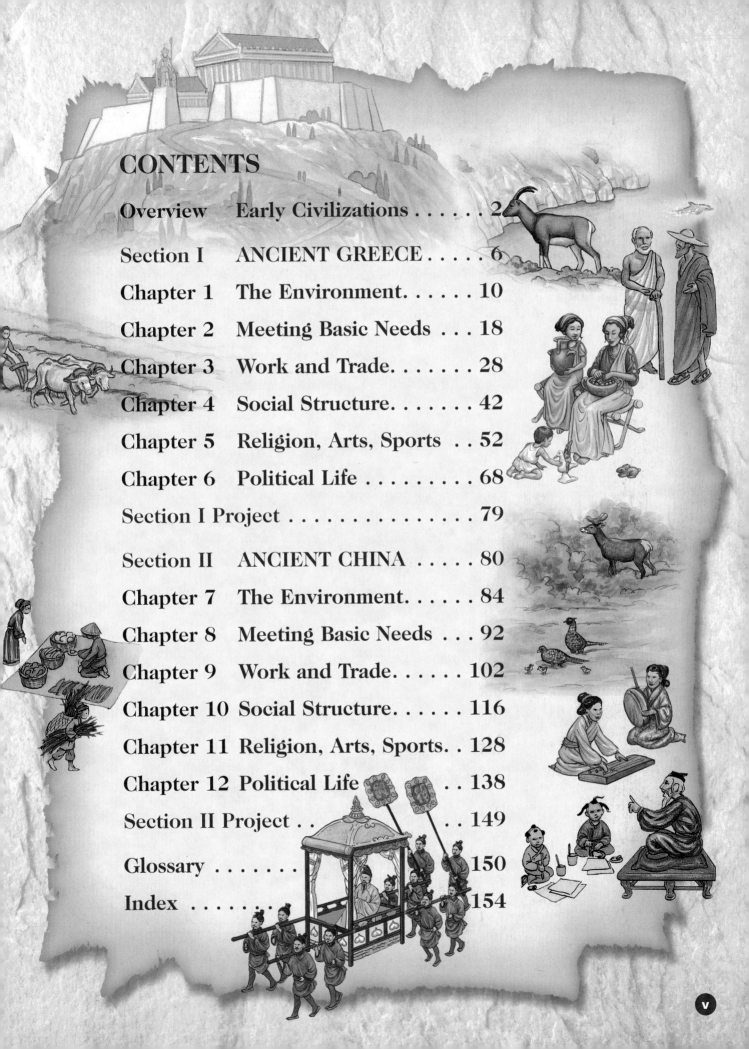

CONTENTS

Overview   Early Civilizations 2

Section I   ANCIENT GREECE 6

Chapter 1   The Environment. 10

Chapter 2   Meeting Basic Needs . . . 18

Chapter 3   Work and Trade. 28

Chapter 4   Social Structure. 42

Chapter 5   Religion, Arts, Sports . . 52

Chapter 6   Political Life 68

Section I Project 79

Section II   ANCIENT CHINA 80

Chapter 7   The Environment. 84

Chapter 8   Meeting Basic Needs . . . 92

Chapter 9   Work and Trade. 102

Chapter 10 Social Structure. 116

Chapter 11 Religion, Arts, Sports. . 128

Chapter 12 Political Life . . 138

Section II Project 149

Glossary 150

Index 154

Overview
Early Civilizations

In ancient times, groups of people lived in many different parts of the world. Certain groups became very successful and powerful. We study these groups to learn about people's ways of life in the past. We also study ways that early civilizations influenced modern life. This map shows some civilizations that existed between 7000 and 2000 years ago.

Ancient Rome
The Roman Empire covered a huge area. The Romans built large cities, roads, huge stone bridges, and stone channels to carry water.

Mississippi/Ohio Valley
The Adena and Hopewell peoples built ceremonial mounds that were centres where many communities met.

The Mayan Empire
The Maya carved inscriptions on huge stone monuments. They wrote detailed accounts of events on animal skins or in books made of bark.

Peoples of the Andes
The Chavin people were the first of many groups to build cities and monuments in the Andes Mountains. They had a large trading network.

North America

ROCKY MOUNTAINS

St. Lawrence

Mississippi

ADENA

APPALACHIANS

Atlantic Ocean

Central America

MAYA

Caribbean Sea

Pacific Ocean

Amazon

CHAVIN

ANDES

South America

Atla Oce

Ancient Greece
The Greeks were great thinkers who are said to have invented democracy. They created remarkable works of art and architecture.

Mesopotamia
The people in Mesopotamia built the first cities, used the wheel, the plough, a system of arithmetic, and an annual calendar.

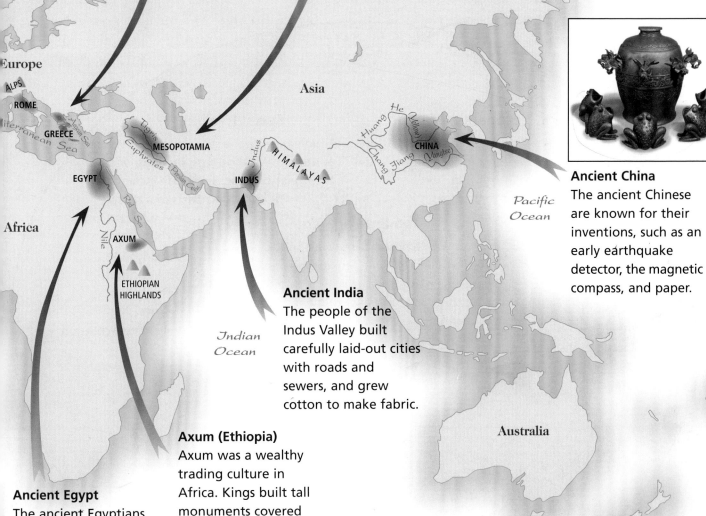

Europe

ALPS

ROME

Mediterranean Sea

GREECE

EGYPT

Africa

Aegean Sea

Tigris

Euphrates

Persian Gulf

MESOPOTAMIA

Red Sea

Nile

AXUM

ETHIOPIAN HIGHLANDS

Indus

HIMALAYAS

Asia

Huang He

Chang Jiang

Yellow

Yangtze

CHINA

INDUS

Pacific Ocean

Indian Ocean

Australia

Ancient China
The ancient Chinese are known for their inventions, such as an early earthquake detector, the magnetic compass, and paper.

Ancient India
The people of the Indus Valley built carefully laid-out cities with roads and sewers, and grew cotton to make fabric.

Axum (Ethiopia)
Axum was a wealthy trading culture in Africa. Kings built tall monuments covered with writing and images above their burial chambers.

Ancient Egypt
The ancient Egyptians learned how to control the floodwaters of the Nile River to irrigate their crops in the dry season.

Ancient Civilizations

When we study a group of people from the ancient past, we look at what they left behind. We study their **artifacts** and stories about them. Artifacts are objects and evidence of how people of the past lived.

Groups that were highly organized and wealthy often built large public buildings, roads, and cities. Many groups had a form of writing and wrote down some of their ideas. We often refer to the **cultures** of these groups as **civilizations**. We can study the culture of a group from ancient times. A culture is a people's way of life. It includes all the ways the people meet their needs.

A Model for Learning about Civilizations

Historians seek to learn about and understand groups of people from the past. They look at four categories of information about a group's culture. The model on this page will help you organize your study of a civilization.

Economic Life

People have to meet their physical needs if they are to survive. Many needs are met by interacting with the environment to make a living. **Economic life** includes the following parts of a culture:

- food
- homes
- clothing
- health
- occupations
- technology
- trade

The Environment

The **environment** refers to the surrounding air, land, and water of a place. People in a place interact with their environment in order to survive. The environment influences their lives. People also change their environments. The environment of a place includes the following:

- landforms
- bodies of water
- climate
- vegetation
- animal life
- natural resources

Social Life

People have to meet needs that relate to their thoughts, feelings, and their relationships. **Social life** includes the following parts of a culture:

- social structure
- family
- language
- education
- religion
- arts
- sports/recreation

Political Life

People have to meet needs that relate to living together as a group. They need to organize and manage themselves and make decisions for the group. **Political life** includes the following parts of a culture:

- political structure
- government and citizenship
- the legal system
- defence and war

Using the Model

The ship diagrams shown below are used as reminders of the Model. They show the three parts of a culture and the environment. A ship diagram appears on the first page of each chapter. The part of the culture on which the chapter will focus is highlighted.

A diagram of a Greek warship called a **trireme** is used as a reminder in the six chapters about ancient Greece. The reminder in the chapters about ancient China is a large sea-going ship called a **junk**.

Remember that a ship will not move without all of its parts. Also, every ship moves within the environment—the water and air. The parts of a culture and the environment relate to each other in the same way.

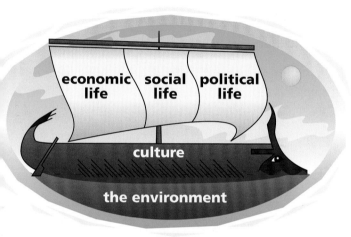

Greek trireme model

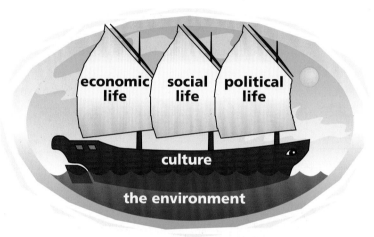

Chinese junk model

Studying History

Many civilizations had thousands of years of recorded history. That is, events in the lives of the people of the past were written down or shown in visual arts, and we can study them today.

History often includes stories from the **oral tradition** of a people. Before writing was common, the stories of the past were memorized. They were passed from adults to children in myths, legends, poems, and songs.

Artifacts and physical evidence of ancient places also give us information about the lives of people from long ago.

Archaeologists excavate (dig up) places to find evidence of how people from early civilizations lived.

SECTION I
ANCIENT GREECE

The ancient Greek civilization developed where modern Greece is today. The ancient Greeks had a written language, the ability to construct large public buildings, and busy trade with many places.

The people of ancient Greece lived in cities and governed themselves. They produced great written works and beautiful pieces of art. These works affected how modern cultures developed.

The history of civilization in the area around Greece is very ancient. In this textbook, we will focus on the period of Greek history from about 500 BCE to 300 BCE. This was the period in which Athens (now the capital of Greece) was more powerful than the other Greek states.

Dates that include BCE (Before the Common Era) run backward in time from the year 1. Dates that include CE (Common Era) run forward in time from the year 1.

Section I Project BUILDING A HISTORY WALL

As you study ancient Greece, you will use the Model for Learning about Civilizations on pages 4 and 5 to build a History Wall of the civilization of ancient Greece.

Prepare for your project by forming groups of 4 or 5. Each group will need a section of mural paper approximately 1 m x 1.5 m in size and paints or markers. Groups will need space to work and store their murals. Each group will build a mural that can be displayed and presented to others.

As you learn about the environment and the economic, social, and political life of ancient Greece, you will illustrate key information on your wall to show how these parts of the culture worked together.

Throughout this section of the textbook, you will be given reminders and suggestions for completing your History Wall.

Locating Ancient Greece

Ancient Greece was not a single country with one government. Many communities and cities over a large area spoke the Greek language. They were usually **independent** of each other. They had separate governments but similar ways of life.

In ancient times, mainland Greece covered an area of about 78 000 square kilometres. It was a little larger than the province of New Brunswick. There were many scattered groups of Greek islands in the Mediterranean, Aegean, and Ionian Seas.

Bodies of salt water almost surrounded the mainland of Greece. Places that are surrounded on three sides by water, like the Greek mainland, are called **peninsulas**.

Greece had settlements and controlled lands in other places. These **colonies** of Greece were considered to be Greek lands. They included many towns on the island of Sicily and in southern Italy. There were also Greek cities in Egypt and what is now Turkey. Greek settlements and bases for trading were found as far away as the Black Sea, Portugal, and North Africa. (Compare the map on this page with the map on the next page to locate these colonies.)

Other parts of the region around the Mediterranean Sea were controlled by the people of Phoenicia, the Persian Empire, and the Etruscans, who lived in northern Italy.

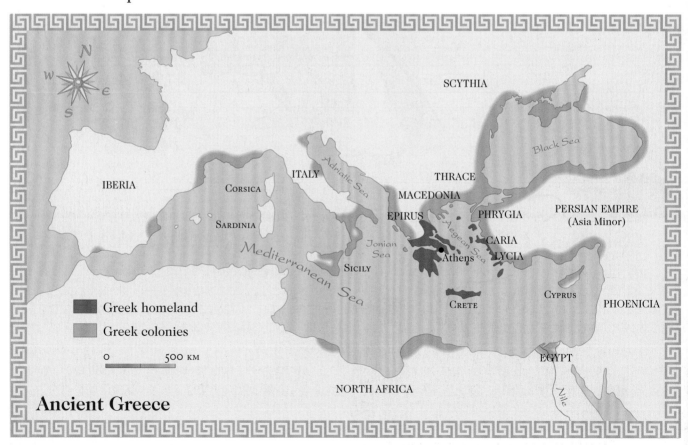

Greek homeland
Greek colonies

0   500 KM

Ancient Greece

Greece Today

Greece no longer has colonies scattered around the Mediterranean region. The land controlled by modern Greece is only slightly larger than the ancient Greek homeland.

The city of Athens is the capital of Greece today.

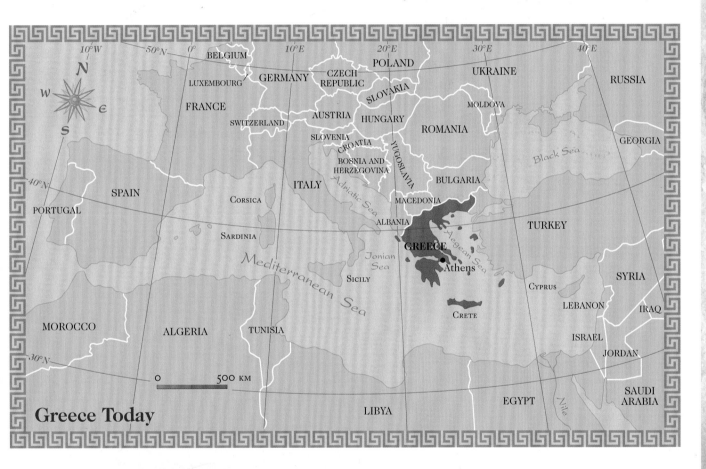

Greece Today

Greek fishing villages today benefit from tourism as well as fishing.

Do ⊠ Discuss ⊠ Discover

1. On an outline map of ancient Greece, locate and label important places and bodies of water shown on the map of ancient Greece on page 8. Include a legend and compass rose on your map.

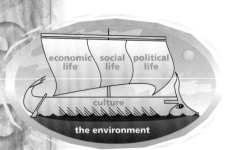

economic life · social life · political life
culture
the environment

Chapter 1
The Environment

The **environment** is the natural surroundings in a place. It includes landforms, bodies of water, climate, vegetation, animal life, and natural resources. The environment influences the ways that people meet their needs. This influences the ways their culture develops.

Focus on Learning

In this chapter you will learn about
- the environment of ancient Greece
- the landforms and bodies of water of Greece
- reading for information
- the climate of Greece
- the vegetation and animal life of Greece
- natural resources found in Greece

Vocabulary

environment	precipitation
irrigation	elevation
climate	natural resources

Landforms

The physical environment of Greece has changed very little since ancient times. Two plates of the Earth's crust push against each other there. Over millions of years, this movement has caused mountains to push up and volcanoes to erupt. Greece today has a rugged and mountainous landscape.

The many islands of Greece are undersea mountains whose tips rise above the water.

Mount Olympus is the highest mountain in Greece (2934 m).

The coastline of Greece, where the land meets the sea, is jagged. Bays and inlets indent the shores. Some places where the sea cuts into the land provide protected harbours for fishing villages.

About half of the land in Greece is rocky and nearly bare of vegetation. The soil on the mountains is thin and stony. The lower slopes of mountains, hills, and plains have places with more fertile soil.

The rusty red colour of the soil is caused by traces of iron.

Some bays have sand beaches, but many are surrounded by rocky cliffs.

An Old Story

When making the world, the Creator first made the great land masses of Europe, the Americas, Africa, Asia, and Australia. The Creator was using a sieve to spread out the soil evenly around the world. Soon, there was a big mass of pebbles, grit, and bits and pieces left in the sieve, but very little soil. The Creator shook the bits and pieces of stone and grit out into the Mediterranean Sea, where they became the Greek islands.

– traditional Greek story

Bodies of Water

The peninsula of Greece is almost surrounded by seas. Water from seas cannot be used for drinking or for **irrigation** (watering crops) because it is salty. However, many kinds of fish and sea life are found in salt water. The seas were an important source of food for the ancient Greeks.

Rivers are an important source of fresh water.

The seas were also important to the ancient Greeks for transportation. Mountains made travel around Greece difficult. Often the best way to move people and goods from one place to another was to go around the coast or from island to island by boat.

Some Greek islands are so rugged and rocky that there are few safe harbours.

Rivers and lakes provide a freshwater habitat for many fish and waterfowl.

Fresh Water

Fresh water is necessary for people, animals, and plants to survive. Greece has few large lakes, and its rivers are rather short. These rivers bring fresh water to the lower valleys and plains.

Many parts of Greece have no year-round rivers or streams. Springs and wells bring fresh water from underground. The ancient Greeks depended on all these sources of fresh water.

Do ⊠ Discuss ⊠ Discover

1. a) With a partner, review the information from pages 11 and 12 and the illustrations on pages 6, 7, and 10. Identify and list key words that describe the environment of ancient Greece.

   b) Discuss how this kind of environment might affect the lives of early Greeks.

   c) Create a title page in your notebook for Section I. Show the environment of Greece.

Reading for Information

The chapters in your textbook are designed to help you to understand early civilizations. The guidelines below can help you to better understand and remember the information in the chapters you will be reading.

Before you read:
- Look at the chapter title page for clues to what the chapter is about.
- Skim through the chapter and read the sub-headings.
- Look at pictures, charts, or maps and read the captions.
- Read the introduction to the chapter.
- Ask yourself questions and make predictions about the topics covered by the chapter.

While you are reading:
- Form a picture in your mind of the main idea that is being described and the details that support it.
- Pay attention to the sequence (order) of the ideas you are reading about.
- Think about how ideas or facts are similar or different.
- Think about descriptions of causes of events and effects that events have.

When you finish reading:
- Discuss with a partner or in a small group what you have learned.
- Use notes, sketches, or graphic organizers (like a web) to help you to organize facts in your mind. Summarize your learning and put your summary in your notebook.

Do ⊠ Discuss ⊠ Discover

1. Read pages 11 and 12 again for information. Make notes, sketches, or a graphic organizer to show the main idea, sub-topics, and supporting details.

Climate

Canada is found between 42°N and 83°N latitude.

Ancient Greece had a **climate** that was very similar to the climate of today. The climate of a region is its weather patterns over a long period. Climate includes average temperatures, amounts of **precipitation** (rain or snow), wind patterns, humidity, and seasons.

Sea breezes blowing along the Greek coasts can make the temperature feel cooler.

Greece has long, hot, dry summers. The blue summer skies are nearly cloudless. There is little rain in summer, so many rivers and wells become dry.

Summer temperatures and lack of precipitation make much of Greece very dry.

Winter is cooler and wetter. Most of the rainfall occurs in the winter. Snow is rare in the Greek lowlands, but it sometimes falls in the high mountains.

The location of a place compared to the Equator affects its climate. Greece is located between 35°N latitude and 41°N latitude. It is much closer to the Equator than Canada.

Climate is also influenced by **elevation**. Elevation is the height of a place above sea level. Parts of Greece are near sea level and others are high in elevation. Generally, places at high elevation, such as mountain tops, are cooler than those at sea level.

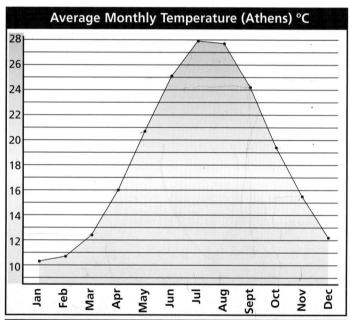

Average Monthly Temperature (Athens) °C

Average Monthly Precipitation (Greece) mm							
Jan	62.0	Apr	23.0	Jul	6.0	Oct	51.0
Feb	37.0	May	23.0	Aug	7.0	Nov	56.0
Mar	37.0	Jun	14.0	Sep	15.0	Dec	71.0

Do ⊠ Discuss ⊠ Discover

1. What does the line graph tell you about the average temperatures in Athens?
2. Use the data on this page that shows the average monthly precipitation in Greece to create a line graph in your notebooks. Share your graph with a partner and check each other's work.

Vegetation

The natural vegetation of Greece has changed little since ancient times. The growth of modern cities and pollution may have affected some plants that grew there.

The climate, soils, and fresh water of a place affect what plants will grow. At the highest elevations on mountains, only lichens, mosses, and low-growing plants are found.

Coniferous trees such as cyprus, pine, and fir grow on mountain slopes where there is soil and water. Deciduous trees such as oak, beech, maple, elm, and chestnut will grow on lower slopes where soil is deeper and there is more water.

Greece is hot and dry most of the year. Low shrubs of laurel, oleander, and wild olive grow well in dry conditions. Plants with leathery skins that conserve water, called succulents, are plentiful in Greece.

The dark, narrow shapes of cypress trees contrast with the silvery-leafed olive trees.

The dry climate of much of Greece means vegetation is often sparse and scrubby.

Coniferous trees grow on mountainsides in Greece where there is enough soil and rainfall.

Pines, poplars, and olive trees can grow on rocky slopes and plains where the soil is not very good. Some trees and plants have large roots that extend deep into the earth to reach water during dry periods.

Many beautiful and fragrant flowers and herbs grow in Greece. Anemone, poppies, and cyclamen can grow at fairly high elevations. Flowers and herbs strong enough to grow in dry, rocky soil include bellflowers, grape hyacinths, thyme, and yarrow.

Bright red poppies grow wild in many parts of Greece.

Animal Life

Animals of many kinds roamed in the woods and countryside of ancient Greece. Mountain lions, brown bears, foxes, wildcats, wild boars, deer, antelope, and badgers were all found there. A few of these animals are not common in Greece today. Others are still found in natural areas.

Pelicans are large, fish-eating marine birds.

In the skies overhead, many kinds of birds are still plentiful. Owls, hawks, eagles, nightingales, turtledoves, partridges, storks, pheasants, and pelicans are just some of the birds found in Greece.

Mackerel, tuna, sponges, squid, shellfish, eels, and dolphins live in the seas. Octopus hide among the undersea rocks, seals live in sea caves, and turtles come onto shore to lay their eggs. The ancient Greeks depended on sea life as a source of food.

Bees and other insects are busy among the flowers. Honey has been gathered as food in Greece from the most ancient times. Many kinds of honey are flower scented.

Many kinds of fish and sea life are found in the seas around Greece.

Natural Resources

Natural resources are the materials found in an environment that people use to meet their needs. The environment of ancient Greece did not have large amounts of useful resources.

Fish, animals, and birds were used by ancient Greeks for food. Most natural vegetation was sparse and scrubby. The ancient Greeks used it as pasture for goats and other animals. Very little of the land was fertile. However, they grew crops wherever they could in the red soil.

The pattern of vegetation on this hillside is formed by ancient fields and olive groves.

Silver, lead, iron, and some copper were mined in Greece. A type of metamorphic rock called marble was used for building and to make sculptures. Clay was taken from the ground to make pottery. Clay pottery was fired in a kiln to make it hard and waterproof.

Do ⬥ Discuss ⬥ Discover

1. Explain in a paragraph in your notebook how plants and trees have adapted to survive in a hot, dry climate.

2. Discuss with a partner how differences in elevation affect the climate and vegetation of Greece.

Using Your Learning

Knowledge and Understanding

1. Use a chart like the one shown below to predict how the environment may have influenced the way ancient Greek civilization developed.

Environment	Description	Influences
Land		
Bodies of Water		
Climate		
Vegetation		
Animal Life		
Natural Resources		

EXAMPLE

2. Design a travel brochure for Greece to include in your notes.

3. Begin a Vocabulary File. Use a file box with alphabetical index cards (or create a computer file) to store your vocabulary words. Give each word a definition, and then sketch a visual reminder of the word. File your words alphabetically.

Inquiry/Research and Communication Skills

4. Using the library, the Internet, or other sources, find additional information about the environment of Greece. Make point form notes about the information you locate.

Application

5. Re-read the information about vegetation on page 15. Work with a partner to create a vegetation diagram. Draw an imaginary Greek mountain, valley, and seacoast. On the diagram, show types of vegetation that grow at different elevations and in different types of soil.

6. Create a postcard to send from ancient Greece to a friend. On the front, illustrate one or more of the characteristics of the environment. On the back of the card, explain why the illustration represents the environment of ancient Greece.

7. Create your own picture symbols to represent the animal life and natural resources found in ancient Greece. Place the symbols on an outline map of ancient Greece. Include a legend for your map.

Section I Project

To begin your History Wall mural, review the key information that you learned about the environment of ancient Greece in Chapter 1. Decide what information you need to include about the environment of Greece. (Hint: the sub-headings in the chapter can help you.) Plan how you will share the task of illustrating the environment of ancient Greece as a background for your History Wall mural.

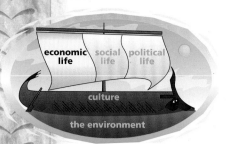

economic social political
life life life
culture
the environment

Chapter 2
Meeting Basic Needs

People need food and water to survive. They also need homes for shelter and clothing to protect them. People also need to maintain good health. Meeting these basic physical needs is part of **economic life**. Most economic needs are met from the environment.

Focus on Learning

In this chapter you will learn about
• how the environment enabled the ancient Greeks to meet their basic needs
• what foods they ate and how they obtained their food
• making notes
• homes in ancient Greece
• ancient Greek clothing
• health care for ancient Greeks

Vocabulary

economic life	brazier	chiton
export	bronze	himation
import	aqueduct	fabric
staple foods	gymnasium	

Food

The ancient Greeks obtained food from their environment by farming, fishing, hunting, gathering, and trade.

They grew fruit trees, including fig, pomegranate, apple, and pear trees. Olive trees produced both black and green olives. Olives were used to make olive oil. Olive oil was produced in large quantities and **exported** from Greece to other places.

♀ LEGACY

The word for water in Greek was "hydro". What English word beginning with "hydro" means water power?

Grapes were grown as fruit, dried to make raisins, or pressed to make wine. Peas and lentils, onions, garlic, and cabbage were also grown.

...esh figs, pomegranates, grapes, fresh dates, ripe olives, ...d dried dates were produced in ancient Greece.

The Greeks raised chickens for eggs and goats for milk and cheese. They grew barley and wheat to make bread and a kind of porridge. There was not enough fertile land to grow as much grain as they needed. Some grain was **imported** from other places.

Goat cheese and bread were important foods for the ancient Greeks.

Along the coast, fish were plentiful and inexpensive. The Greeks enjoyed many types of seafood, such as lobster, shrimp, mussels, and octopus.

Fresh herbs such as thyme and bay leaf were gathered from the environment and used to flavour food.

Meat was not plentiful because it was expensive to raise animals for food. There was not enough grain grown for all of the people's needs. The small amount of good land was used for crops, not for pasture. Some people hunted for deer, wild boar, and hares. Most people only ate meat at special feasts or banquets.

The Greeks had no sugar. Honey was used for sweetening foods, and people liked sweet fruits such as figs and raisins. Wine mixed with water was served at meals as a beverage. Poorer people often drank goat's milk or water instead.

Daily Meals

Most Greeks ate two meals a day. At midmorning, they ate bread dipped in wine and water, followed by beans or peas and raw onion or a roasted turnip. Meals were often eaten outdoors.

The main meal was eaten at sunset. This meal consisted of bread or porridge, cheese, figs, olives, and fish if it was available. These were the **staple foods**. Staple foods are basic foods that are eaten almost every day.

This large pottery container was called a *kylix*. Men who were feasting together drank wine from it.

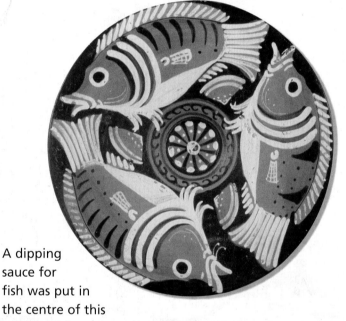

A dipping sauce for fish was put in the centre of this pottery dish.

Women and slaves prepared all of the food. Cooking was done on a charcoal hearth (like a barbecue pit) or on a grill over coals in a metal pan called a **brazier**. Food containers and utensils were made of **bronze** or fired clay. Bronze is made from a mixture of metals, mainly copper and tin.

A few drops of wine were poured out on the ground as an offering, to show respect and thankfulness to the gods and goddesses.

Aqueducts

Drinking water was scarce in such a dry climate. Some people had a well in the courtyard of their home. Others had to go to public fountains to obtain water. A city might build an **aqueduct** to bring fresh water from a lake or river to the public fountains and wells. An aqueduct is an artificial channel built to carry water across hills and valleys. Aqueducts were even cut through barriers like mountains.

Do ⊠ Discuss ⊠ Discover

1. In your notebook, write a daily menu for a family. Sketch and label the foods in your menu. Underneath, describe where and how the Greeks would have obtained the food and beverages.

2. In a paragraph, describe how the environment of ancient Greece helped provide for the people's basic need for food. Include ways their environment limited what they ate.

Note-making

Note-making is a way to summarize information. Summarizing helps you learn and remember main ideas. To make notes, you need to identify the topic and the sub-topics that support it. Then you need to add details that are important to those ideas.

A web is one way of making notes. A web is a type of graphic organizer for arranging and recording information visually. This makes it easier for you to understand the topic as a whole and see how the ideas are connected.

To make a web:

- Begin with a circle or shape in the middle of your page. Write a title for your main topic in this space.

- Make branches to join your main topic to circles or shapes where you can write your sub-topics. Sub-topics identify important parts of the main topic.

- Use more branches to connect each sub-topic to its details. You might want to draw pictures to show some of the information on your web.

- Continue to connect ideas that relate to the information on your web. If items on one branch are related to items on another branch, you can draw lines to show that they are related.

Dairy Products

Fruits + Vegetables

Food in Ancient Greece

Breads + Grains

Beverages

Meats + Fish

Do ⊠ Discuss ⊠ Discover

1. Make notes in your notebook to summarize the information on page 20 about daily meals.

Homes

Homes in ancient Greece were built from materials found in the environment. Most homes had a number of rooms that surrounded a central courtyard.

To keep the houses cool and shady, there were few windows. In winter, charcoal was burned in metal braziers for warmth.

Homes were lit with lamps like the pottery one on the left, which burned olive oil. A bronze lampstand such as this one would have belonged to a very wealthy family.

Men and women usually lived in separate parts of the house. Slaves had separate living space from the family.

A few early Greek homes had bathtubs. Most men went to the **gymnasium**, a public sports complex, which had steam baths. Women and children often bathed in bronze basins.

Smaller homes usually had a bedroom, a living room with a fire pit for cooking and warmth, and a storage room.

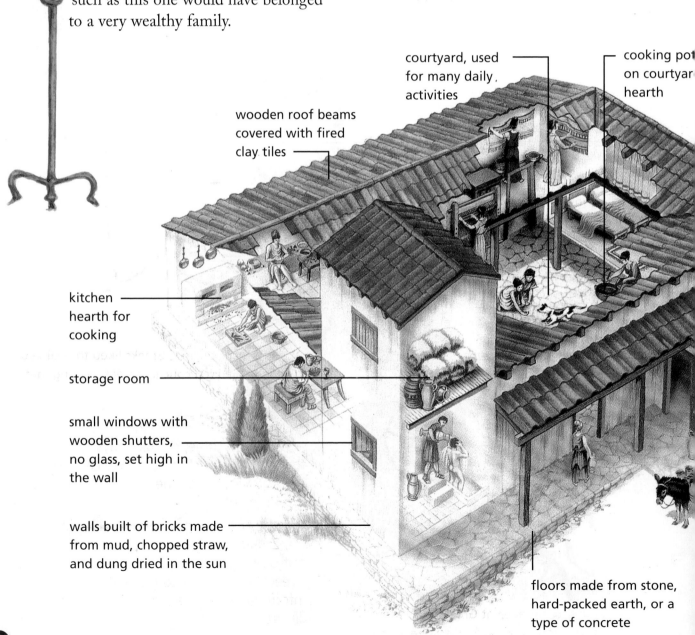

courtyard, used for many daily activities

cooking pot on courtyard hearth

wooden roof beams covered with fired clay tiles

kitchen hearth for cooking

storage room

small windows with wooden shutters, no glass, set high in the wall

walls built of bricks made from mud, chopped straw, and dung dried in the sun

floors made from stone, hard-packed earth, or a type of concrete

Furniture

The Greeks did not have a lot of furniture in their homes. Pieces of furniture were often carried into the courtyard during the day.

Stools with folding legs were common, but chairs were also used in wealthy homes. Stools and tables with three legs didn't wobble as much on uneven earth floors.

Beds were wooden frames with leather straps stretched across them to support a mattress and cushions.

A man and woman are seated together on a bench at a banquet.

Possessions were hung on the walls or stored in baskets and chests.

The Greeks made furniture from wood, leather, and fabric. Sometimes furniture was decorated with inlaid ivory or metal.

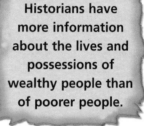
Historians have more information about the lives and possessions of wealthy people than of poorer people.

The ancient Greeks liked to recline on padded couches to eat evening meals.

A woman of ancient Greece sits in front of an open door holding a hand mirror.

Do ⊠ Discuss ⊠ Discover

1. In groups of three, discuss ways that the homes in ancient Greece were influenced by the environment.

2. Use the information on pages 13, 18, 22, and 23 to help you make notes on homes in ancient Greece. Remember to include information provided in the text, illustrations, and captions.

Clothing

The main garment worn by the people of ancient Greece was called a **chiton**. A chiton was a large rectangular piece of finely woven cloth. It was wrapped around the body like a tube and pinned over the shoulders.

In cool weather, a wool cloak called a **himation** was worn over the chiton. Both men and women wore hats to protect them from the heat of the sun.

Sandals and boots were made from leather to protect the feet on stony ground or in wet weather. Poor people went barefoot much of the time.

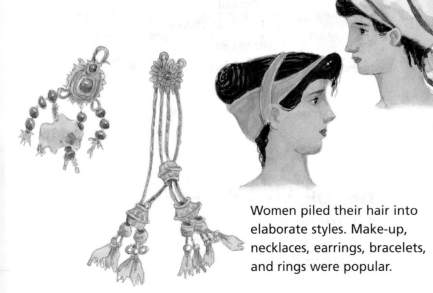

Women piled their hair into elaborate styles. Make-up, necklaces, earrings, bracelets, and rings were popular.

Workers and children wore shorter chitons, or they pulled the fabric up over their belts to keep it out of the way.

Weaving

Chitons were usually made out of fine wool or linen cloth. The Greeks raised sheep for wool. The wool was spun into thread and then woven into cloth. They grew flax for making linen. Expensive silk imported from Asia was used to make clothing by those who could afford it.

Women in ancient Greece took pride in their weaving. **Fabrics** were woven on looms made of heavy wooden beams. The looms were set up permanently in the home. All girls learned to spin and weave. Most of the fabric used by their families was woven at home. Women also supervised women slaves doing some of the weaving.

Dyeing

Dyes were made from natural substances from the environment. Some special colours had to be obtained from other places by trade. These dyes were more expensive.

Cloth was prepared for dyeing by soaking it in a chemical called alum to keep the colour from washing out. Then the cloth was put into a vat of dye. It was stirred gently so that the cloth would absorb the colour. Finally, the cloth was rinsed in cold water and dried.

Saffron yellow was a favourite colour, and purple, red, and violet were also fashionable.

> The best purple dye came from a small sea snail found near Tyre in Phoenicia. It was so expensive, only the most wealthy could afford it.

Sources of Natural Dyes	
Colour	**Source**
Yellow	stalks of the weld plant
Deep pink	roots of the madder plant
Brown	bark of the oak tree
Blue	fermented dried leaves of the woad plant
Purple	a type of sea snail
Violet	an insect larva called the kermes worm

Do ⊠ Discuss ⊠ Discover

1. Discuss with a partner how clothing in ancient Greece was suitable for the climate.

Health

The Greeks valued health and physical fitness. Young men trained vigorously to serve in the army or navy. Women needed to be healthy to have strong children.

Greek people did not live as long on average as modern people do. This was because babies and infants often died of childhood diseases. Women frequently died in childbirth. Young men were often killed when fighting in wars.

This doctor is taking the pulse of his patient and asking him to describe his symptoms.

The Greeks thought that sickness was a punishment from the gods. When they were ill they asked Aesculapius, the god of medicine, for a cure.*

Sometimes patients went to a temple for a night to sleep and dream of a cure. They would describe their symptoms to a priest at the temple. The priest would treat them and prescribe herbs, exercise, and baths. The priests of the god Aesculapius had much practical experience and skill at treating illness.

Greek doctors used instruments made of bronze and iron (such as the ones below) to perform surgery. They used drugs such as opium and mandrake, a powerful herb, for anaesthetics. Operations were very dangerous.

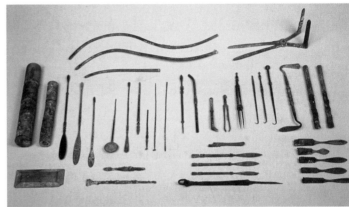

Hippocrates (460–377 BCE)

Hippocrates was a famous doctor who lived in ancient Greece. He wrote many books about medical subjects. He believed that illness in a part of the body was related to the health of the whole person. For centuries, many doctors swore the Hippocratic oath. They promised to always work to save lives.

---

*The pronunciation guide on page 150 will help you pronounce the Greek words and names.

Using Your Learning

Knowledge and Understanding

1. Make a web in your notes like the one shown below. Complete the web to show how the ancient Greeks met their basic needs.

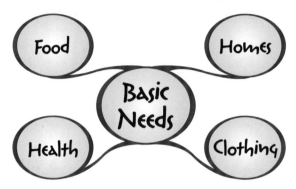

2. Add the vocabulary words from Chapter 2 to your Vocabulary File. Remember to include a definition and a sketch for your word.

Inquiry/Research and Communication Skills

3. Use an encyclopedia or other sources to find information about how dyes for colouring fabrics are made today.

4. Prepare a flyer to distribute with an imaginary ancient Greek newspaper. Your flyer should advertise food, clothing, furniture, and real estate.

5. Find out more about Hippocrates in the library or on the Internet at www.encyclopedia.com/html/h/hippocra.asp or www.bbc.co.uk/schools/gcsebitesize/sosteacher/history/36373.shtml. With a partner discuss why you think that Hippocrates is considered the "Father of Modern Medicine."

Application

6. Imagine you are stranded on a deserted island. Write a story about your adventure explaining how you will meet your basic needs.

7. Make a chart to compare the way that the early Greeks met their basic needs with the way that these needs are met in your culture.

economic life social life political life

culture

the environment

Chapter 3
Work and Trade

People do work in order to meet their needs and to get things that they want and enjoy. When people produce a **surplus** of something—more than they need for themselves—they can **trade** this surplus for things from other places. Work and trade relate to the economic part of their culture.

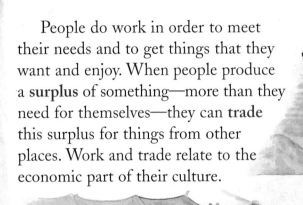

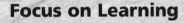

Focus on Learning

In this chapter you will learn about
• the economic life of ancient Greece
• how their work enabled the Greeks to meet their needs
• farming, fishing, and mining in ancient Greece
• how craftspeople and merchants contributed to meeting basic needs
• trade between the Greeks and people of other places

Vocabulary

surplus	terraces	agora
trade	technology	apprentice
slave	aquaculture	vendor
public works	quarry	

Economic Life in Ancient Greece

Farming was the most important occupation in ancient Greece. People who owned large amounts of land were usually wealthy because people in cities depended on landowners to produce their food.

This terracotta (fired clay) sculpture shows a farmer ploughing with two oxen.

Coins were often kept in a small pottery container.

Occupations

Some other occupations in ancient Greece included fishing, mining, and working as artisans and craftspeople. Merchants were involved in trade. Business people provided their customers with products and services that they needed. Other people worked in the arts, education, religion, and government.

Most women worked mainly in the home. Women were essential to economic life. They cooked, raised children, and wove fabrics.

Slaves

Slaves were an important part of the economic life of ancient Greece. Slaves were people who were owned by another person, a business, or the government. Most slaves were captured in wars or were the children of slaves.

Slaves worked on farms, as servants in homes, as workers in factories, as shopkeepers, as entertainers, in the mines, and as crew members on merchant ships. Slaves could be forced to do whatever their owners wished. They could be sold to other owners.

Slaves that belonged to the government worked on public works projects that were for the benefit of all the people. Examples of public works are roads and aqueducts.

Slaves with owners who treated them fairly had a better life than others did. Most slaves were not paid for their work. Sometimes skilled slaves could earn enough to buy their freedom. Some owners also gave slaves their freedom as a reward.

Slaves were given new names by their owners.

Standing looms are still used in Greece today to make rugs and fabrics.

Do ⊠ Discuss ⊠ Discover

1. Work with a partner to list two questions about work in ancient Greece that you would like to have answered in this chapter. You will come back to these questions at the end of the chapter.

Farming

The majority of the men of ancient Greece were farmers. Some wealthy families owned large farms and had many slaves to work on them. Most farmers worked with their family members.

The environment of Greece was mainly steep hills, mountains, and small areas of plains. Farmers had to use whatever land was available. The Greeks built **terraces** like stair steps on hillsides to give them more room for planting. Terraces also helped prevent the winter rains from eroding, or washing away, the soil on the hills.

In most places, the soil was rocky and difficult to prepare for growing crops. The long, hot dry summer affected what crops farmers could grow. Each year, they planted part of their land and let the remaining part rest.

Grain was stored in bins or barns. Farmers sold their products at the market in the nearby town or city. Grain was transported in large pottery jars or baskets carried by donkeys.

Women on farms probably worked mainly in the home. They prepared food, raised families, spun thread, and wove cloth. On small farms, women and children probably helped in the fields when needed.

Farm Products

Wheat and barley were grown on the best land. The Greeks planted their grain crops in October, just before the winter rains began. Most of the year was hot and dry. Irrigation was often needed to bring water to crops.

Rockier hillsides were used to grow olive trees and grapevines. Grapes were harvested in September. Many other fruit and vegetable crops were ready at the same time of year.

Some farmers kept bees in hives. They produced honey from wild flowers and the blossoms of fruit trees. Goats were raised for milk and cheese, chickens for their eggs, and sheep for their wool.

Farming Technology

Technology means the tools and skills of a group of people. The Greeks used irrigation to bring water to their fields in the hot, dry summers. They dug canals to manage the flow of water. Inventions like the Archimedean Screw (shown below) were used to raise water to a higher level.

A Greek called Archimedes invented a machine like a screw to raise water. This type of technology is still used in some parts of the world to irrigate dry land.

Farmers mostly used simple wooden and metal tools. Oxen or mules pulled wooden ploughs, sometimes with iron tips on the blade. Seeds were dropped by hand into the furrows left by the plough. Hand sickles like this one on the right were used for cutting grain. Grain was harvested in May.

Olives were harvested in December by beating the branches with sticks.

Olive oil was produced by pressing fresh green olives in a simple press weighted with stones.

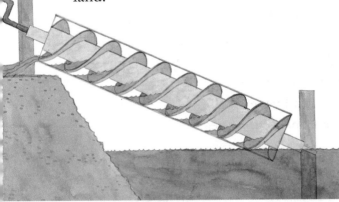

Archimedes (died 212 BCE)

Archimedes was a famous scientist and mathematician. Besides his irrigation pump, he is known for an important scientific principle. If a solid object is put into a liquid, some of the liquid will be displaced (pushed out of the way). In the story told about this, he sat down in a bathtub full of water and noticed that water poured out over the sides. He did experiments later to confirm his results. Some other accomplishments of Archimedes included:

- studying levers and pulleys for lifting huge weights
- inventing a war machine like a catapult
- positioning mirrors in the harbour to confuse attacking navies

Do ⊠ Discuss ⊠ Discover

1. With a partner, discuss why terracing was used in ancient Greece. In your notes, illustrate terracing and list the ideas you discussed.

Fishing

Fish were plentiful in the seas around Greece. Small fishing villages were scattered around the coast of the Greek mainland and islands.

Fishing was usually a family activity, not a large business. Most fishers were not wealthy, but they made a living.

Greek fishers used small wooden boats to fish offshore. They used woven nets and bronze fishing spears to catch mackerel, tuna, octopus, squid, shellfish, and eel. They caught lobsters in cages made of twigs. They also fished with a pole and line and bronze fish hooks.

Fish and seafood were sold fresh to people who lived near the coast. They were also dried or packed in salt or oil to preserve them. Preserved fish could be traded to other places.

Greek Fishers Today

Fishing is still an important part of the Greek economy, although fish are not as plentiful as in the past. Over the years, pollution and over-fishing of the seas have decreased the fish population. Today, Greek coastal vessels and trawlers fish the waters of the Mediterranean. A large Atlantic fleet gathers fish from the Atlantic Ocean. Greece also has an **aquaculture** industry. Aquaculture is a process by which both marine and freshwater fish are raised in tanks and ponds.

Fishers work along the seacoasts catching many types of seafood.

Mining

The ancient Greeks mined the earth for ore containing metals. These included iron, silver, lead, gold, and copper. Copper and tin were mixed to make bronze. Bronze was an important material for making metal tools and objects.

This ceremonial axe-head is made of bronze. It was donated to a temple of the goddess Hera by a butcher.

The Laurion Mine

The ancient Greeks discovered a source of ore containing both silver and lead at a place called Laurion, near Athens.

The Laurion mine belonged to the government of Athens. Mining was done by slaves captured in wars. They had to work for up to ten hours a day in the underground tunnels. In the 5th century BCE, there were about 20 000 slaves working in the silver/lead mine at Laurion. Because lead is poisonous, slaves who worked in the mine often died after a few years.

Stone Quarries

Cutting stone from a **quarry** is another form of mining. A quarry is a surface mine where blocks of stone are cut from solid rock. The marble and other types of stone the Greeks used in their buildings and sculptures came from their mountainous environment.

Blocks of stone are cut from solid rock in quarries.

In some places, the miners had to crawl along the narrow tunnels and lie on their backs to work.

Ancient Greek artisans produced delicate jewellery like these earrings from precious metals such as gold and silver.

Do ⊠ Discuss ⊠ Discover

1. In small groups, identify natural resources that the Greeks used to meet their economic needs.

   a) List these resources and give examples of how the Greeks used each resource.

   b) Decide which resource you think was the most important. Explain your thinking.

Artisans and Craftspeople

Artisans and craftspeople were skilled workers who made items that people needed or luxuries that they wanted.

Craftspeople were skilled workers who produced items for everyday living, such as tools or sandals. Artisans produced decorative or artistic items, such as pottery or weavings.

Some carpenters made furniture or other household items. Carpenters, stoneworkers, and other builders worked on magnificent public buildings.

An artisan or craftsperson learned the skills of the trade by becoming an **apprentice** as a child. An apprentice worked for an experienced person, usually his father, and learned from him for a number of years. When an apprentice finished training, he had to show his skill, usually by doing a special project. Then he was qualified to work alone. Eventually he might train his own apprentice.

The shoemaker pictured in this *kylix* is working at his craft. He has shoes and leather hanging in his workshop.

Most artisans and craftspeople living in cities had their shops in their homes. Many lived close to the **agora**. The agora was the central public marketplace where most business and many other aspects of life took place.

Potters made beautifully decorated pottery and also simple, useful containers for everyday use.

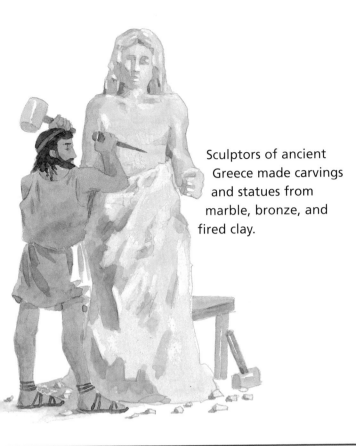

Sculptors of ancient Greece made carvings and statues from marble, bronze, and fired clay.

Leatherworkers made boots and sandals. Metalworkers used silver, iron, or bronze to make jewellery, tools, knives, shields, and armour. Other craftspeople made items like musical instruments or baskets.

The women of Greece were skilled weavers. They produced fabrics of all kinds for clothing, blankets, curtains, and wall hangings.

Most artisans and craftspeople were free men and women. Some were skilled slaves who paid part of their income to their owners. Although few artisans and craftspeople were really wealthy, most made a good living.

Make Greek Pottery

You will need

- modelling clay
- rust, black, and tan paint
- paint brushes
- varnish

1. Make a Greek bowl or plate using self-drying clay.
2. Allow your piece of pottery to dry thoroughly; then paint it a rust colour.
3. While the paint is drying, choose an aspect of Greek life that you would like to show on your piece of pottery.
4. Plan what you will draw; then sketch it on a piece of paper.
5. When the first coat of paint is dry, lightly sketch or trace the drawing onto your piece of pottery.
6. Fill in your sketch with black and tan paint.
7. When this second coat of paint is dry, cover your piece of pottery with a matte (dull finish) varnish.
8. Allow the varnish to dry.
9. Create a class display of Greek pottery.

The Agora

The agora, or marketplace, was an important part of an ancient Greek city. People came there every day to buy or sell, or to relax and meet with friends.

☥ **LEGACY**

What does the English word "agoraphobia" mean?

Farmers, fishers, and craftspeople came to the agora to set up stalls and to sell their products. On the small streets that ran off the agora, many artisans and craftspeople had shops. They worked at producing their goods or met and spoke with customers there.

Vendors sold goods like fabric or silverware. Fast food sellers sold tasty snacks. The Greeks could visit a doctor in the agora, consult a lawyer or politician, listen to a teacher, or attend a public meeting. Many fine buildings and government offices were situated around the agora.

Do ⊠ Discuss ⊠ Discover

Carefully examine the picture of the agora, and imagine that you are part of that picture.

1. a) With a partner, discuss
   - who you are and what you are doing
   - the sounds, smells, and activities you are experiencing
   - the conversations you are having or the purchases you will make
   b) Write a story about your visit to the agora. You may act it out.

Ikaros at the Agora

Ikaros awoke to the loud clatter of horses' hooves and the noisy bustle of the streets. He had overslept. The agora was already humming with activity. Ikaros jumped from his thin mattress and straightened his clothing. He rolled up his bedding and rushed out of the slave quarters to meet Haimon, his master, at the workshop near the agora.

Ikaros had been orphaned as a baby. He might have died of starvation, but he was found by Haimon, a master potter. The potter had raised him with the other slaves belonging to his small business. Now Haimon was training Ikaros as an apprentice potter.

Ikaros felt fortunate to be learning an important craft. His knowledge and skills as a potter would earn him some of his own money. He dreamed one day of buying his freedom. He hoped at least to live in his own room and only pay part of his earnings to Haimon.

For now, he was just an apprentice. In the workshop, he turned the heavy wheels for Haimon and the other potters to fashion urns, bowls, and plates. He kept the kiln heated with wood or charcoal so that the temperature was right for firing. He carefully transferred vessels and clay figures to the kiln to be fired and then removed them after it cooled down.

Ikaros was happy learning the skills of a potter, but he was also curious about everything. He could not attend school like boys his age who were free. However, with the help of an older slave, Ikaros had learned to read and write. He dreamed of discussing great ideas about the world with one of the great teachers who often spoke in the agora.

Today Ikaros was helping Haimon sell their products at a stall in the agora. As the day progressed, the agora became noisier, hotter, and more crowded. When Ikaros noticed a group of citizens had gathered nearby, he became curious. A few minutes later, Haimon sent him to purchase something to eat. Now he would be able to find out what was going on!

Ikaros looked over at the gathering of citizens. There was the great Aristotle! Ikaros went nearer and listened intently as Aristotle described amazing things he had discovered about different kinds of plants and animals.

All at once, Ikaros heard his name being called. Haimon's food! He suddenly remembered his duty. He had forgotten all about Haimon's food because his mind was full of new ideas!

– Danielle Stock

Merchants and Business People

Merchants in ancient Greece were business people who travelled to distant places to buy and sell goods or produce. They would purchase objects and materials that could not be found in Greece. Then they would transport them home and sell them for a profit in the agora. Merchants often had large fleets of trading ships.

Cities in Greece each produced their own coins and money. Sometimes merchants would exchange their money for coins from other cities. Bankers, or money changers, charged a fee for the service of exchanging money. They also loaned money to merchants.

Greek Measurement	
Length	
1 finger	= 19.3 mm
1 foot	= 16 fingers
1 olympic cubit	= 24 fingers
Weight	
1 talent	= 25.8 kg
Volume	
1 metrete	= 39.4 litres

The units of money in Athens were the obol and the drachma. Workers earned an average of half a drachma (or 3 obols) a day. The most common coins in ancient Greece were half-obol, one-obol, one-drachma, and four-drachma pieces.

Money and Measurement

Money and measurement were important for doing business. Merchants, bankers, shopkeepers, and artisans needed to calculate amounts of goods and prices.

Greek Numbers		
I	=	1
II	=	5
⊿	=	10
H	=	100
X	=	1000
M	=	10 000

Do ⊠ Discuss ⊠ Discover

Try these questions using ancient Greek numbers and measurements.

1. a) Estimate how many talents you weigh.
   b) How many fingers make 3 olympic cubits?

2. Make rulers or measuring tapes that measure in the following units; then measure your desk in
   a) Greek fingers
   b) Greek feet
   c) olympic cubits

3. Make up your own question. Have a friend answer it.

Trade

Athens had a large fleet of merchant ships and a powerful navy of warships. Trade between places all around the Mediterranean Sea had been going on for many centuries. Athens controlled much of this trade during the time period of 500 to 300 BCE.

Trade was important to the economy of Greece. The many Greek colonies were connected to the Greek homeland through trade. (The map on page 8 shows where Greek settlements were found at the time that Athens was most powerful.)

Exports

Greece produced a surplus of olive oil and wine. Fine woollen and linen fabrics were also produced for markets outside Greece. The mines near Athens produced valuable silver, and Greek pottery was in demand. The Greeks exported these products to people in other places who wanted them.

These workers in a fabric merchant's shop are weighing goods.

Imports

The Greeks were not able to produce everything they needed from their environment. They had to import some goods. They traded with other places for additional grain and for other products they needed or wanted.

Some products came from places far to the east, such as China and India. Rare and fragile goods and those transported great distances were the most expensive to buy. They also gave the greatest profit to merchants who imported them for their customers.

Main Exports	Main Imports
olive oil	grain
wine	papyrus (paper)
silver	spices
wool & linen fabric	silk
pottery	ships' rigging and sails
marble	ivory

♀ LEGACY

The Greeks established laws for ships at sea. These early laws were the basis for later laws that determine how ships operate on the seas today.

Imports to Greece

Do ⊠ Discuss ⊠ Discover

1. Look at the trading map on this page.

   a) List the places that supplied Greece with grain.

   b) Identify two other goods that were imported and where they came from.

   c) Share your answers with a partner. Think back to earlier chapters; then discuss why the ancient Greeks relied on trading to meet their needs.

Using Your Learning

Knowledge and Understanding

1. Parts of Greek economic life are listed on the chart below. Find examples of technology used for each and describe what they are used for. Put your chart in your notebook.

Economic Life	Technology (Types/Uses)
Farming	
Irrigation	
Fishing	
Mining	
Trade	
Arts/Crafts	

EXAMPLE

2. File the definitions and sketches for your words from Chapter 3 in your Vocabulary File. Include interesting Greek words that you are learning.

3. Refer back to the two questions you developed for number 1 on page 29. In your notebook, write answers to your questions.

Inquiry/Research and Communication Skills

4. Find out about some of Canada's main exports and imports. How are they different from or similar to the exports and imports of ancient Greece?

Application

5. Create a word collage on an outline map of ancient Greece. Think of words that describe what you have learned about economic life in ancient Greece. Write words all over the map. Use colour and interesting letters. Share your collage with another student.

6. Use a graphic organizer to compare technology in ancient Greece with technology in Canada today.

7. Visit the website www.mcs.drexel.edu/~crorres/ Archimedes/contents.html to find out more about Archimedes. Choose a method of sharing your information.

Section I Project

Chapters 2 and 3 focused on economic life in ancient Greece. In your project groups, refer back to the sub-headings and chapter overview pages in these chapters. Discuss what you have learned about the economic life of the ancient Greeks. Identify the key information and plan how you will show this information. Share the tasks of illustrating economic life on your History Wall mural.

economic life · **social life** · political life

culture

the environment

Chapter 4
Social Structure

People in a culture live together in families and communities. This is one way they meet their need to relate to others. They have different roles or jobs and may have different rights. They raise children and help them to learn the knowledge, beliefs, and values of their culture. These are also parts of **social life**.

Focus on Learning

In this chapter you will learn about
- the different groups of people living in ancient Greece
- family life in ancient Athens
- social activities of the Greeks
- language and education in ancient Greece
- role-playing
- Greek philosophers

Vocabulary

social life

social structure

citizen

metic

dowry

philosopher

Social Structure

The people of a culture live and work together in communities. They belong to various groups with different roles, work, responsibilities, and rights. These groups form the **social structure**.

In ancient Greece, the major social groups were citizens, metics, and slaves. In all groups, children contributed by helping their parents.

Citizens

Citizens of Athens were men and women whose parents had been born in that city. Men who were citizens could vote, participate in making laws, and own land. Women citizens could not vote or make laws. In Athens, the citizens were the people with the most power, although not all citizens were wealthy.

Women

Women citizens had some legal rights but little independence. They did not take part in government.

Most women citizens contributed to society by caring for the family and the home. A few, such as priestesses, worked in public positions. Priestesses performed religious duties.

Metics

Metics were free men and women who did not have all the rights of citizens. Many had not been born in Greece. Some were slaves who had been freed. Metics could not take part in government or own land. However, they could become successful through their work. Many metics worked as builders, merchants, and skilled craftspeople.

Slaves

Slaves were men, women, and children who were owned by other people. Most Greek slaves were people captured in wars or children of slaves. They could not vote, own land, or choose their work or where they lived. Many slaves worked as labourers, craftspeople, entertainers, and servants.

Family Life

Greek households usually included a father, mother, and children. Often grandparents or other relatives lived with the family.

The people living in a Greek home had different roles. Fathers were in charge of the family and made most of the decisions concerning the other members. Most men worked to provide for the family's economic needs.

Mothers took care of the home, cared for children, and supervised the household slaves. The number of slaves in a Greek household depended on the wealth of the family.

Children helped in the home or the father's business and learned from their parents.

Marriage

The Greeks believed that it was important to get married and have children. Fathers arranged their children's marriages. The bride's family gave a **dowry**, usually a sum of money, to the man she was marrying to set up the new home. Women married when they were around 14, but men were often twice that age.

Men

Greek men who were not wealthy learned a skill or occupation and spent their lives working at it. Many wealthy Greek citizens spent their days in the agora. They shopped, did business, attended citizens' meetings, or listened to speakers.

Most of a man's social life was spent with other men. Men went out to the theatre and to parties together. They also went to the gymnasium, a public sports complex, to participate in athletic events.

All healthy young men spent several years in military training. This prepared them to join the army or navy. They could be called upon to fight in wars when needed.

Women

Women spent most of their time at home cooking, cleaning, spinning wool, and weaving. They made household items like blankets, pillows, and wall hangings. Women cared for the children and taught their daughters home-making skills. Wealthy women had slaves to help them.

Sometimes a male slave would accompany a woman to the agora to do some personal shopping. Some women left the home for such tasks as carrying home water from a public well.

A woman's social life mainly took place in other women's homes. Women also attended some religious festivals and events such as women's athletic competitions.

Children

Girls stayed at home until they married. Boys were looked after at home until they went to school. In wealthy homes, children were taught by a home tutor, sometimes an educated slave. Children also helped their parents in the home or family business.

Young children in ancient Greece had toys and played games. Most play was a form of practising adult roles. Girls commonly played with dolls and boys practised with toy swords.

A yoyo was a favourite children's toy.

Rolling a hoop with a stick was good for a boy's physical coordination.

Exercise and fun are both basic needs for all people.

Toys were made with materials from the environment. This terracotta doll would have been painted.

Do ⊠ Discuss ⊠ Discover

1. Use a Venn diagram to compare roles of men and women in ancient Greece.

2. Imagine you are visiting a family in ancient Greece. Write a letter to a friend at home about family life in ancient Greece.

A Long Journey

Melika could see Athens from the hill next to the family's farm. The temples on the Acropolis were shining in the early morning sun.

Melika watched her father and the men load the cart with grapes, jugs of wine, fresh vegetables, and a bolt of fine wool fabric. Then her father climbed onto the cart and a slave shouted to the ox. The huge animal kicked up clouds of dust with its hooves as it moved. Her father was on his way to the agora to sell some products and purchase things needed on the farm.

Melika went inside to help her mother. They had spun wool into fine yarn and dyed it a beautiful yellow in a vat in the courtyard. Today Melika would begin to weave a warm himation for her brother.

Before joining her mother, Melika filled a clay bowl with water for her pet bird. She had adopted Nikos as a fledgling when he had tumbled into the courtyard of their house and broken his wing.

Although he was soon able to fly away, Nikos spent part of every day in the courtyard. Melika loved the way he trotted around looking for seeds and insects. Sometimes he chirped to her in a conversational way. She imagined that he was telling her about the world around—the birds, trees, and the paths far away over the hills.

Melika's mother often said crossly that Melika was too old for pets and daydreams. In a few years, she would leave home and have a household of her own to run. She had to learn a woman's responsibilities. Melika sighed a little and set the dish of water by the door.

Nikos didn't appear. Melika worried as she drew the bright yellow wool back and forth on the loom. Perhaps a hungry eagle had caught him.

Late in the afternoon, Melika heard her father enter the courtyard. He said to Melika with a frown, "I found that bird hiding behind a basket of vegetables on the cart when I got to the market this morning."

Melika prepared herself for bad news. She was afraid to ask her father what had happened to Nikos.

Melika's father crossed the courtyard and sat down in the shade. He took off his hat to fan himself. "A merchant at the agora wanted to buy the bird because it was tame. He thought a fine lady might want to buy it for a pet. I thought of selling it, ... but I decided that a lady already owned it, so I brought it back."

Melika looked up at her father, shyly. "Thank you," she said.

"Well," he said, smiling a little, "bring me some wine, daughter. It was a long journey."

Language

Greek was spoken and written in Greek settlements all around the Mediterranean, Adriatic, Aegean, Ionian and Black Seas. People who wanted to trade with the Greeks or travel between Greek settlements learned their language.

The ruler of Cyrene is watching workers pack and load a type of herbal medicine for export to Greece.

Greek writers wrote poetry, plays, and stories about the lives of the people and the gods. Important Greek thinkers, called **philosophers**, wrote about their ideas and scientific discoveries. When people today read works written in ancient Greek, they often read translations. This means that the works have been rewritten in a different language.

♀ **LEGACY**

"Philosophy" includes the name "Sophia." What did this Greek word mean?

There are many English words that originally came from Greek, particularly medical and scientific terms.

Writings from ancient Greece, such as laws that were carved in stone, survive today in museums.

The Alphabet

Each letter in the Greek alphabet represented a sound, just as the English alphabet does. Many English alphabet letters come from Greek. The word *alphabet* is formed from the names of the first two letters in the Greek alphabet, *alpha* and *beta*.

The Greek Alphabet

Capital Letter	Small Letter	Name	Sound
A	α	alpha	a
B	β	beta	b
Γ	γ	gamma	g
Δ	δ	delta	d
E	ε	epsilon	e (as in bed)
Z	ζ	zeta	z
H	η	eta	a (as in bay)
Θ	ϑ	theta	th (as in think)
I	ι	iota	i
K	κ	kappa	k
Λ	λ	lambda	l
M	μ	mu	m
N	ν	nu	n
Ξ	ξ	xi	x
O	ο	omicron	o (as in pot)
Π	π	pi	p
P	ρ	rho	rh, r
Σ	σ	sigma	s
T	τ	tau	t
Υ	υ	upsilon	u
Φ	φ	phi	ph
X	χ	chi	kh
Ψ	ψ	psi	ps
Ω	ω	omega	o (as in dome)

Do ⊠ Discuss ⊠ Discover

1. Compare the Greek alphabet with the English alphabet. Which letters are similar in English?

2. Write a message using the Greek alphabet. Exchange your message with a friend, and translate each other's messages into English.

Education

Boys usually went to school after about age seven, unless their families needed them to work. A male slave usually took the boy to school. The teacher taught reading, writing, mathematics, and music. Some families could afford a private tutor for sons.

Oral tradition for teaching about the past was important in ancient Greece. Students learned to memorize and recite long poems. Poems like Homer's *Odyssey* and *Iliad* told the stories of Greek history and the lives of the gods, goddesses, and heroes. Homer was a famous Greek poet who lived around 800 BCE.

In their teens, boys went to a special school to become physically fit. They learned to wrestle, run, jump, and throw a javelin and discus. Only wealthy boys learned to ride horses, which were expensive to buy and to feed. Some boys continued their studies with a philosopher.

Sons of farmers, fishers, miners, craftspeople, artisans (such as the metal workers shown above), and merchants worked as apprentices to learn the skills needed to do their fathers' work.

Girls learned their mothers' skills and knowledge in the home. Some girls from wealthier families learned to read, write, count, and play a musical instrument such as the lyre, shown below.

A pointed stick called a stylus was used to write on a tablet coated with wax. The wax could be smoothed over and the tablet used again.

Role-play

Role-play is a skill that requires you to take on the personality, the characteristics, the feelings, and the behaviours of another person and to act as that person in a given situation.

Before your role-play:

- Know your character's personality.

- Think about how your character will act in a particular situation.

- Visualize yourself acting in your character's role.

- Practise your role.

During your role-play:

- Keep your character's personality and background in mind.

- Use your voice, facial expressions, and movements to show your character's emotions, ideas, and attitudes.

- Listen carefully to other characters and respond appropriately.

- Use costumes or props to convey your character realistically.

After your role-play:

- Ask for feedback from your teacher and classmates about your performance.

- Think about and discuss your role-play experiences with a partner.

Do ⊠ Discuss ⊠ Discover

1. In groups of three, plan and present a role-play of three people meeting in the agora.

Greek Philosophers

Philosophers were educated men who had studied the physical world and human life. They shared their ideas with students and interested people.

Philosophers believed that it was important for people to reason things out and to solve problems by thinking. They wrote books, taught, and led discussions about their ideas.

Ancient Greek philosophers had many ideas about science, mathematics, and politics that are still considered important today. Their ideas influenced the way many branches of knowledge developed in the centuries after they lived. The three most famous Greek philosophers were Socrates, Plato, and Aristotle.

♀ LEGACY

Aristotle invented a pinhole camera called a "camera obscura." His ideas for taking pictures with light eventually led to the television and movies we have today.

Plato had many ideas about good government.

Aristotle developed a classification system for grouping plants and animals into categories.

Socrates' method of teaching was to ask difficult questions that caused people to think and explore new ideas.

Do ⊠ Discuss ⊠ Discover

1. In groups of three, discuss reasons why philosophers were important in ancient Greece. Identify two reasons and then add them to your notes.

Using Your Learning

Knowledge and Understanding

1. Draw illustrations to represent the main ideas about the social structure of ancient Greece. Write captions for your illustrations and include them in your notes.

2. Make file cards with definitions and sketches for each of the Chapter 4 vocabulary words. Include cards for the Greek words you have learned. File your words alphabetically.

3. The Greeks enjoyed word puzzles like acrostics. The first letter of each clue spells the final answer of an acrostic. Create an acrostic word puzzle for one of the vocabulary words you have learned. Trade with a partner and solve each other's puzzles.

Inquiry/Research and Communication Skills

4. Research meanings for the English words below, which come from the Greek language. As a class, make a bulletin board display, illustrating the words and showing their meanings.

- geography
- history
- telephone
- microscope
- hypodermic
- theatre
- gymnasium
- agoraphobia
- ostracize
- symposium
- drama
- philosopher
- athletics
- marathon
- stadium
- rhapsody

5. Using the library, the Internet, or other sources, find out more about any ancient Greek philosopher. In your notes, write a biography for the philosopher you choose. (See page 123 for ideas on writing a biography.)

Application

6. In small groups, develop a skit demonstrating the lives of people in ancient Greece. Make sure that you include the various groups in the social structure and show something about their lives. Perform your skit for another group.

7. Imagine that you are a boy or girl living in ancient Greece. Write diary entries for two days describing some of your typical daily events.

Chapter 5
Religion, Arts, Sports

Religion, the arts, and sports are related to social life. People's beliefs, feelings, and sense of wonder about their world are expressed in their religion and in their arts. People also need to interact with one another and have fun. One of the ways the ancient Greeks met these needs was through sports.

Focus on Learning

In this chapter you will learn about
• ancient Greek beliefs
• visual, literary, and performing arts in ancient Athens
• architectural accomplishments of the Greeks
• decision-making
• athletic competition in ancient Greece

Vocabulary

shrine	mythology	frieze
temple	legend	capital
sacrifice	quest	columns
oracle		

Religion

Religion was an everyday part of the lives of the ancient Greeks. They worshipped many gods and goddesses and celebrated festivals in their honour. There was often a small **shrine** in the courtyard of the home. It was used for family offerings to the gods and goddesses.

Temples and Shrines

The Greeks built **temples**, which are large public buildings used for religious purposes. At religious festivals, the people often walked to the temple in a procession. They sang songs and brought offerings.

A valuable farm animal like an ox was often led in the procession. The animal was blessed and given to the god or goddess as a **sacrifice**. It was killed by the priests of the temple, then the meat was cooked and divided among the worshippers.

Oracles

The people believed that they could learn about the future from the gods. They went to an **oracle** for advice. An oracle was a shrine with a priest or priestess who was believed to foresee the future. There was a famous oracle

at Delphi on Mount Parnassus. (See the map inside the back cover of the book to find Delphi.)

Sometimes answers given by an oracle could be interpreted in more than one way. If things didn't happen as expected, it could be said that the oracle's answer had not been interpreted correctly.

Part of a temple of the goddess Athene can still be seen at Delphi.

The Underworld

Greeks believed that the god Hermes led a dead person's soul to the Underworld. A ferryman named Charon then transported the soul across the river Styx to the Underworld in his boat. Relatives placed coins on the eyelids of a dead person as payment for the ferryman. Providing food for the journey was often part of a funeral ceremony.

Do ⬙ Discuss ⬙ Discover

1. Discuss why you think a farm animal would have been a suitable sacrifice to the gods. Relate your answer to the ways Greeks met their basic needs.

2. a) Write a question that might have been asked at the oracle of Delphi.

   b) Exchange questions with a partner, and write a possible response for your partner's question. Does it have more than one meaning? How else might it be interpreted?

The Olympians

The Greeks thought that the most important gods and goddesses lived on Mount Olympus, the tallest mountain in Greece. Olympian gods and goddesses had different interests and roles.

The Greek word **mythology** refers to the traditional stories told about the gods and goddesses and about how their behaviour affected humans. Myths often tell a story of how something in the natural world came to be, such as how the world was created. Many myths also try to teach people something about right and wrong.

Zeus was the chief god, the ruler and law giver. He was associated with the sky, storms, thunder, and lightning.

Hera was the goddess of marriage and childbirth. Women sought her blessing if they wished to have children.

Poseidon was the god of the sea. He is often shown holding a trident, a three-pronged fishing spear. Poseidon was also associated with horses.

Demeter was the goddess of farming, crops, and the fertile earth. She is also remembered as a sorrowing mother. She searched the world for her daughter Persephone, who was stolen by Hades, the god of the Underworld.

Apollo was the god of light, beauty, and youth. He was associated with prophecy (telling the future), music, poetry, philosophy, healing, and medicine. He is often shown carrying a musical instrument called a lyre.

Athene was worshipped as the goddess of wisdom and war. She was the protector of Athens and was associated with the olive tree and the owl.

Artemis was the goddess of hunting, the forests and hills where she hunted, and wild animals. She is often shown carrying a bow and arrows.

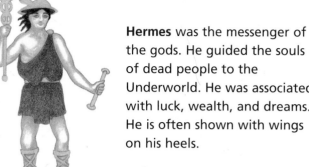

Hermes was the messenger of the gods. He guided the souls of dead people to the Underworld. He was associated with luck, wealth, and dreams. He is often shown with wings on his heels.

Hephaestus was the god of fire, the blacksmith god. He was an artisan who made beautiful and powerful things for the gods and goddesses and for humans. He was physically handicapped but very strong.

Hades was the god of the Underworld, where he ruled the world of the dead.

Aphrodite was the goddess of love and beauty. She had a son called Eros (Cupid) who was also associated with the power of love.

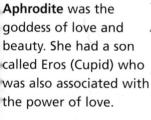

Hestia was the gentle goddess of the hearth and home. The hearth fire was a symbol of protection and warmth for the ancient Greeks.

Ares was the god of war. The Greeks sought his protection when they went to fight wars.

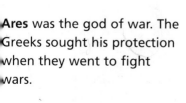

Do ⊠ Discuss ⊠ Discover

1. Design a crest for one of the Olympian gods or goddesses showing his or her interests and roles.

Demeter and Persephone

Demeter, the goddess of crops and fields, was very important to the people of the world. She blessed the crops and encouraged the earth to produce abundant food, herbs, and flowers.

Demeter had a daughter named Persephone who was very dear to her. Demeter would watch Persephone dance among the flowers that she loved, and her heart would be filled with tenderness. Demeter's joy made the crops even more fruitful and generous.

One day Persephone was walking in a field of breeze-blown flowers. She turned and bent to touch a nodding red poppy.

Suddenly, a huge crack appeared in the earth. A chariot pulled by snorting black horses burst out of the chasm. It carried Hades, the God of the Underworld. He grasped the startled girl by the wrist and pulled her up beside him. They whirled and descended back under the earth, which closed up behind them.

Hades, the god of the Underworld, had fallen in love with the beautiful Persephone. He vowed to have her for his wife. He thought she would be happy to rule beside him as Queen of the Underworld. He did not think of any other consequences of his actions.

Demeter searched the world over for her lost daughter. No one seemed to know where she was. She grieved, and her sorrow affected the whole world. She no longer blessed the crops, and the plants of the earth became dormant and would not grow.

The people of the earth were desperate. Crops failed and children went hungry. Demeter no longer heard their prayers, so they appealed to Zeus to help them. Zeus sent a message to Hades that Persephone had to be released.

Hades knew that if Persephone ate any food while in the kingdom of the dead she would be doomed to stay there. He offered her a pomegranate. She was hungry, but ate only a few of the glistening red seeds. However, it was enough to bind her to the Underworld.

In the end, Hades obeyed Zeus and let Persephone return to her mother. Demeter was overjoyed to see her, and immediately the plants of the earth began to awake and grow.

"Alas, mother," Persephone said to her, "each year I will leave you again for a few months, because I have eaten the food of the Lord of the Underworld. But I will always return."

Thus, each year plants become dormant and sleep for the winter, and every spring the new shoots reach up their green leaves to the sun.

The Arts

The ancient Greeks appreciated beauty, good design, and artistic expression. Greek artists and artisans created many beautiful objects and artworks. Many have been found by archaeologists and preserved in museums.

Greek writers created works of poetry, philosophy, history, and plays that are still read and performed today.

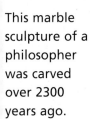

The perfume container above is 6.8 cm high. It is carved with a lion head and decorated with armed warriors and racing horses.

Visual Arts

Skilled artists and artisans in ancient Greece made beautiful decorated pottery, statues, and carvings. Scenes from Greek life or stories of the gods, goddesses, and heroes were popular subjects of art.

Most humans shown in Greek art are ideal (perfect) forms rather than realistic, imperfect people. The Greeks felt that having a perfect, healthy, athletic body was to be most like the gods.

The porch of one of the temples in Athens is held up by marble statues of women called caryatids.

The war horse and its keeper above are part of the carved marble panel called a **frieze**. This frieze decorated the Parthenon, a temple in Athens.

This marble sculpture of a philosopher was carved over 2300 years ago.

Do ⊠ Discuss ⊠ Discover

1. Look at the examples of Greek art on this page. Discuss with a partner what you can learn about life in ancient Greece from these examples.

Literary Arts

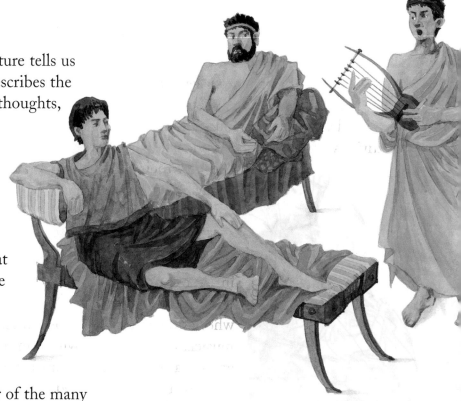

Ancient Greek literature tells us about their culture. It describes the ways people lived, their thoughts, and how they felt about historical events or the ways people behaved.

The Greeks enjoyed telling and listening to stories. Poetry was popular at festivals and at men's dinner parties. The poet recited aloud. He often played a stringed instrument called a lyre at the same time.

The Greeks were the first people in the Western world to have libraries that could be used by all of the people.

Only a small number of the many written works from ancient Greece have survived until today. These were written by hand on papyrus or parchment. Papyrus was made from a plant fibre. Parchment was made from thin sheets of animal hide. Both become brittle and crumble with age.

Few copies of writings existed. They were passed from person to person and recopied. If all the copies disappeared, the written work was lost forever. Sometimes we know a book existed because other authors refer to it in their writing.

"The ruins of himself! now worn away
With age, yet still majestic in decay."

In *The Odyssey*, the poet Homer describes Odysseus' first sight of his father, who had grown old while Odysseus was lost at sea.

Sappho

Sappho was a Greek poet. She lived on the island of Lesbos and her writing was respected and admired. She recited her poetry to audiences. People throughout the Greek-speaking world bought books of her poems. They could even buy a small portrait of her as a souvenir. Only two short poems and some lines quoted by other writers have survived to this day. Nevertheless, she is considered to be one of the ancient world's great poets.

Myths

Myths are stories that usually refer to supernatural beings or events. Greek myths describe the personalities and activities of the gods and goddesses and how their behaviour affected humans.

Orpheus was a character in Greek mythology whose skill as a musician was so great that the wild creatures would gather to listen to him.

Fables

A fable is a brief story that gives a moral or a lesson. Aesop was a Greek slave who wrote many animal fables that are still read today. One of Aesop's most familiar fables is "The Tortoise and the Hare." A hare was so confident that he would win a race against a tortoise that he lay down for a rest. He woke to discover with dismay that the tortoise was at the finish line.

Legends

Legends are stories linked with real people and real events. One famous Greek legend tells about Jason and the Argonauts. Jason's uncle took the throne of the kingdom from his father. The uncle feared that Jason would be a threat to him, so he sent Jason on a **quest** to search for the Golden Fleece. He was sure that Jason would not succeed in the quest or even return alive from this dangerous task.

Jason gathered a group of heroes to sail with him on his ship, the *Argo*. He had many adventures. Eventually, he rescued the Golden Fleece while the dragon guarding it was asleep.

Do ▧ Discuss ▧ Discover

1. In your library find and read some Greek myths, fables, or legends. Choose a scene from one of these stories. Prepare a skit or tableau to share with the class.

2. In small groups, discuss the meaning of a quest.

Performing Arts

Going to the theatre to see plays was an important part of life for the ancient Greeks. Many theatres were built and hundreds of plays were performed. Mostly men attended plays at the theatres.

Theatres were shaped like bowls. The rows of seats were built like steps on the slopes of hillsides. Ancient Greek theatres were so well designed you could hear a whisper on the stage even from the very top seats.

The large mouth on a Greek mask acted like a megaphone to make the actor's voice louder so he could be heard farther away.

The theatre at Epidauros has been restored and is still used today.

A few actors played all of the main parts in Greek plays. They often played more than one part. Male actors played both the female and male roles. There was also a chorus of actors who spoke and moved together.

The actors wore masks to show which character they were playing. The facial expressions of the masks could be seen from a distance. Actors switched masks as they changed roles. There were different types of masks for plays that were comedies and for serious plays called tragedies.

Entertainers

Poetry and plays were not the only kinds of performing arts in ancient Greece. People also enjoyed being entertained by jugglers, tumblers (gymnasts), dancers, and singers. Male and female entertainers were often hired to perform at banquets and parties.

Music

Music was popular in ancient Greece. People sang at weddings, funerals, and births. They had love songs and battle songs, religious songs and party songs. There were many musical instruments, including the lyre and a kind of double flute.

Do ⊠ Discuss ⊠ Discover

1. With a partner, discuss the terracotta figures of actors shown above. Do you think they are acting in a comedy or a tragedy? Why?

Make a Greek Theatre Mask

You will need

- 1 m string
- modelling clay
- papier mâché strips
- petroleum jelly
- ruler and scissors
- diluted white glue
- glue or glue gun
- paint (acrylic works best)

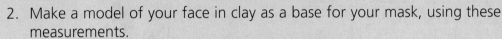

1. Measure your face so your mask will fit. Wrap a piece of string (or tape measure) around your face to measure the circumference.

2. Make a model of your face in clay as a base for your mask, using these measurements.

3. In the correct places, build a nose and lips, and hollow out the eyes.

4. Cover the clay model with a thick layer of petroleum jelly.

5. Use layers of papier mâché strips to build a mask on the clay model. Use extra layers to build up places like eyebrows and lips.

6. Allow the mask to dry until it begins to pull away from the clay base.

7. Remove the mask carefully. Use extra strips to add details if necessary. Make holes for the eyes, nostrils, and mouth. Dampen the mask first if it is too dry.

8. Brush the mask with diluted white glue to strengthen it.

9. Allow the mask to dry thoroughly. Punch holes on each side for the string to pass through.

10. Paint the mask. If desired, add decorations, false hair, or details with glue or a glue gun. (An adult must help you when you work with a glue gun.)

11. Cut the string in half and tie one piece to each side through the holes. These can be used to tie on the mask or to hang it up for display.

Architecture

Many beautiful temples and other public buildings were built in ancient Greece. They were paid for by wealthy citizens or from wealth acquired through war.

Architects designed public buildings to be magnificent. This made the people proud of them and impressed strangers. Because temples were homes for gods and goddesses, they were built to be grand and beautiful.

Columns and Capitals

A special feature of these structures were the **columns**, the pillars that supported the roofs. Most Greek houses had flat roofs, but public buildings often had peaked roofs. There were no domes or spires, which were developed in later centuries. Many pillars were needed to support the roof of a large public building like a temple.

The carved top ends of columns were called **capitals**. The styles were different in different parts of Greece. Greek public buildings were also decorated with marble or bronze carvings and statues. These were often covered with colourful paint or gold.

The Doric, Ionian, and Corinthian styles of capitals can be identified on different columns today.

Features of Greek architecture are still used in public buildings and monuments today. This building is Osgoode Hall in Toronto.

Do ⊠ Discuss ⊠ Discover

1. Look at the picture of Osgoode Hall in Toronto on the left. How is it similar to Greek buildings? Identify the style of capital on the columns used for the building.

Decision-making

The skill of decision-making helps you choose an appropriate action when there are different points of view about a question or issue. It involves examining the values and consequences of each possible choice and choosing the best one.

Decision-making Model

1. **Understand why a decision is needed.**
   What is the issue, and why should a choice be made?

2. **Gather accurate information so that you clearly understand the issue.**
   Research the facts.

3. **Think about a number of possible alternatives (choices).**
   Take a survey of opinions; brainstorm choices as a group.

4. **Evaluate the choices by considering the possible values and consequences of each.**
   List the alternatives. List pros and cons (positive values and negative consequences) of each.

5. **Select the most appropriate choice.**
   One method is to prioritize them from "most appropriate" to "least appropriate."

6. **Explain the reasons for your choice.**
   How did the values outweigh the consequences?

The Parthenon was the main temple in a complex built over 2400 years ago. The temple honoured the goddess Athene. The people of Athens believed Athene protected them and made them wealthy.

The main building material was marble. The frieze around the top showed a religious procession in honour of the goddess. Men, women, horses, chariots, and sacrificial animals were carved in marble to form this frieze.

Parts of the Parthenon are still standing. Earthquakes, wars, thieves, erosion, and pollution have damaged it over the centuries since it was built. The people of modern Greece work to preserve what remains of it. Many tourists visit the Parthenon each year.

Over a hundred years ago a British Ambassador, Lord Elgin, visited Greece. He got permission to take sculptures and pieces of the Parthenon's frieze back to England. The British Museum in London has had these pieces in their collection of art and artifacts since then. They are often called the Elgin Marbles. They are carefully preserved in special displays. The British Museum is used as a resource by scholars and visited by many tourists.

Many people in modern Greece want the works of art to be returned to Greece. They feel they belong there and want to put them in a Greek museum.

Do ▨ Discuss ▨ Discover

1. a) In small groups, use the decision-making model on page 63 to examine the issue of whether the Elgin Marbles should remain in England or be returned to Greece.

   b) Present your decision and your reasons to the class or write them in your notes.

Sports

The ancient Greeks enjoyed athletic competition. They believed that the gods were pleased by demonstrations of physical fitness and athletic skill. It was important for men to be fit because they could be called to fight in wars at any time.

The stadium at Delphi seated 7000 people. Sixteen runners could line up in the starting blocks.

Male citizens of Athens visited the gymnasium daily for physical activities. They took part in many athletic contests to honour their gods.

Women had athletic competitions in honour of the goddess Hera. Running was the only women's event.

The Spartan Girl

This small bronze sculpture portrays a Spartan girl running a race. Sparta was a Greek city-state that was often at war with other city-states. All of the young people trained hard to be physically fit, although only men fought in the military. Girls of Sparta were expected to be fit and healthy so their children would grow up to be good soldiers.

The Olympic Games

Several athletic competitions drew athletes from all over Greece to compete. Messengers travelled to all major cities to announce when the competitions were to occur.

These games were so important that wars between regions would stop so that competitors and spectators could travel safely to the competitions.

The Olympic Games were held every four years in a place called Olympia in southern Greece. They honored the god Zeus. The games lasted for five days, and only men attended them.

There were fewer events than in today's Olympic games. The major events were horse and chariot racing, boxing, wrestling, and the pentathlon. The pentathlon was a series of five contests: long jump, discus, javelin, wrestling, and running.

At the time of the ancient Greeks, wrestling was good training for soldiers.

In the final event of the Games runners raced in full armour. Winners were awarded garlands made of olive leaves. After five days the games concluded with a banquet and offerings to Zeus.

The Modern Olympic Games

The Olympic Games continued until the 4th Century CE. Over the centuries, earthquakes and floods destroyed the original site of Olympia. About 200 years ago, the buried site was found by archaelogists.

The first modern Olympic Games were held in Athens in 1896, over a century ago. People hoped that having a modern Olympic Games would promote a more peaceful world.

A stadium used in Athens about 330 BCE was rebuilt and used for the first modern Olympic games in 1896.

The Olympic Games are a huge international event.

There were 10 000 contestants who came from 198 different countries to the Sydney Summer Olympics in 2000 in Australia. Millions of spectators watched events in 28 different sports.

During the 1988 Winter Olympics in Calgary, the men's cross-country race took place at the Canmore Nordic Centre.

Canadian high-jumper Debbie Brill competed at the 1976 Olympics in Montreal.

Do ▧ Discuss ▧ Discover

1. a) The rings on the Olympic flag represent unity among the nations of Africa, the Americas, Asia, Australia, and Europe. How does this symbol represent unity? Why do you think the rings are coloured blue, yellow, black, green, and red?

   b) Draw the Olympic flag in your notes and describe its symbolism.

Using Your Learning

Knowledge and Understanding

1. Think about the religious beliefs of the ancient Greeks. How did these beliefs influence the culture? Write your ideas in your notes.

2. Imagine you are sending news to a friend about your study of social life in ancient Greece. Be sure to include 3 to 4 facts. Use one of the following for your message:
   - drawing, with caption
   - letter
   - e-mail message
   - postcard
   - story

3. Complete definitions and sketches for the vocabulary words in this chapter and any Greek words you've found. Put the words in your Vocabulary File.

Inquiry/Research and Communication Skills

4. Using the library, the Internet, or other sources, find myths or legends from another culture. Use a Venn diagram to compare one of these with a Greek legend.

5. Visit the website www.aesopfables.com and read some of Aesop's Fables found on this site. Make a list of the lessons they teach.

Application

6. Design a building based on Greek architecture. What is the building's purpose? What modern features will it need and what features will be based on Greek architecture?

7. Olympic athletes take an oath promising to commit themselves to the ideals of good sportsmanship in competition. What does sportsmanship in competition mean? Make a T-chart showing the difference between good sportsmanship and poor sportsmanship.

Section I Project

Chapters 4 and 5 focused on the social life of ancient Greece. With your group, review the sub-headings in these chapters. Identify the key information about social life to be illustrated on your History Wall mural. Share the tasks of illustrating it.

Chapter 6
Political Life

People develop ways to organize and manage themselves so they can live together as a group. They have ways of making decisions for the community. This is their **political life**. It includes their method of government, the laws they make for living together peacefully, and their interactions with groups from other places.

Focus on Learning

In this chapter you will learn about
- creating a map
- Greek city-states
- Greek colonies
- different types of governments
- democracy in ancient Greece
- the ancient Greek legal system
- group discussion
- defense and war between city-states

Vocabulary

political life	democracy
city-state	public official
state	administration
tribute	ostracize
dictator	hoplite
hereditary monarchy	phalanx
oligarchy	

Creating a Map

1. Decide what area your map will show.

2. Use an atlas or other sources of maps to find a reference map for the location you need.

3. Decide what part of your reference map you will need. For example, you may wish to make a map of Greece but your reference map shows all of Europe. You only need to copy the portion that shows Greece.

4. Sketch or trace an outline of the portion of the map that you need onto your page. If necessary, enlarge your map using a photocopier.

Greece Today

5. All maps need to provide certain general types of information. Use lines, labels, colour, and symbols to show the following:
   - boundaries
   - important areas (e.g., provinces, geographic regions)
   - names of places
   - physical features (e.g., bodies of water, mountains)
   - names of physical features

6. Decide what other specific information your map needs. Examples of specific types of information are
   - trade routes
   - trade products
   - vegetation or animal life

7. Your maps will also need a title, legend, compass rose, and latitude and longitude.

City-States

Ancient Greece was not a single country as it is today. Communities were separated from one another by the mountainous environment and the sea. Many independent **city-states** were established on the mainland and the Greek islands.

In ancient Greece, cities and their surrounding countryside were called city-states. They did not belong to a larger political unit like a country. They made their own laws and managed their own affairs. In political life, the **state** is the main political unit. It is independent and has its own government.

The Greek city-states shared a similar language and culture. They traded with one another, but they also went to war with one another to try to increase their land and power.

A city-state's strength and power were based on trade, success in war, and taxes. Sometimes they united to defend themselves against outside political powers.

The map on this page shows some of the Greek city-states at the time when Athens was powerful. There were many more than shown here.

♀ **LEGACY**

The English word "politics" comes from "polis," the Greek word for city-state. Find English words that relate to the Greek word "polis."

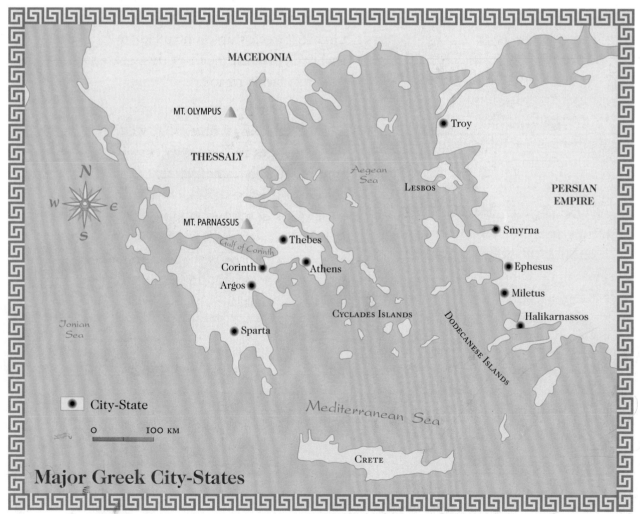

Major Greek City-States

City-states that had been conquered by a more powerful city-state were forced to pay a yearly tax called **tribute**. This increased the other city's wealth and power.

Athens

The city of Athens had a population of around 250 000 people. Another 250 000 people lived in villages and farms in the surrounding countryside. The city was built around an old walled fort on the Acropolis hill.

By the 4th century BCE, Athens was the wealthiest and most powerful of the city-states. It had many allied city-states and received tribute payments and taxes from others. The Parthenon was built on the Acropolis to celebrate the Greek victory over Persia.

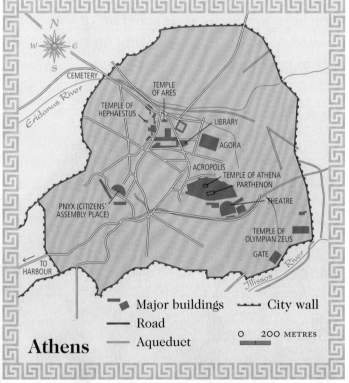

Athens

Key:
- Major buildings
- Road
- Aqueduct
- City wall

0   200 METRES

The Acropolis can still be seen in modern Athens.

Greek Colonies

As the population of Greece increased there was not enough fertile land to grow food for all of the people. City-states appointed men called founders to sail in search of new, more fertile lands and start colonies, or settlements. These colonies were under the control of the city-state.

Greek colonies were established in Sicily, Italy, Egypt, around the Black Sea, and as far as away as Iberia (now Spain and Portugal) and North Africa. (See the map on page 8 to locate these colonies.)

The new colonies were governed by Greeks. They traded with the Greek homelands and increased the wealth of Greece. Greek ships controlled travel and trade around much of the Mediterranean region.

Greek settlers in other lands established communities that were like the city-states in Greece. Most of these communities became centres of Greek culture and learning. The settlers built their cities near the sea and grew crops of grain and vegetables. They sent products back to Greece and imported items they needed from Greece. They also traded with their non-Greek neighbours.

Do ⌧ Discuss ⌧ Discover

1. Follow the steps on page 69, Creating a Map, to make a map in your notes showing the extent of Greek colonization. Use the map on page 8 of this textbook as your reference. Be sure to label the places mentioned on this page on your map.

Government

Governments make decisions about how countries will be managed. They also make laws so that people can live together peacefully. There are different ways that countries may be governed.

Types of Government

A government in which one very powerful person takes control and makes decisions for all of the people is called a **dictatorship**. Many Greek city-states were dictatorships.

In a **hereditary monarchy** a king or a queen governs by right of birth. An **oligarchy** is a type of government where a small group of people has all of the power. Oligarchs may be elected, appointed, or they may take power by force.

The ancient Greeks in Athens were the first people to establish a form of government called **democracy**. In democracies today, both men and women are citizens and there are no slaves. Citizens can all vote to elect representatives who make decisions for their country.

Democracy in ancient Greece was similar in some ways to modern democracy. However, it was really a "limited democracy" because citizenship was restricted. Only free men and women whose parents had been born in the city-state could be citizens. Women were not able to take part in government. Metics and slaves were not citizens.

Democracy in Athens

The government in Athens was made up of the Assembly and the Council.

The Assembly

All male citizens of Athens were members of the Assembly. Members of the Assembly took turns being judges, Council members, and **public officials** (people with government jobs).

Limited Democracy in Athens

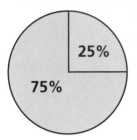

25%

75%

Only 25% of the people of Athens took part in political life.

☐ participated in government
☐ did not participate

Members of the Assembly voted to make laws and decide on important issues, such as whether the army would go to war. The Assembly met once a week on a hill near the Acropolis. A minimum of 6000 citizens had to be present for the Assembly to meet.

When too few citizens showed up for an Assembly meeting, guards were sent out to collect the number that was needed.

At Assembly meetings the citizens would speak about their ideas. They voted by a show of hands on matters that were important to them.

Speakers in the Assembly were timed with a water clock to make sure they did not talk too long.

The Council

The Council had representatives from each of the ten regions in Athens. Each region selected 50 men and a military general to be on the Council. The ten generals were the city's most important officials.

The Council was responsible for carrying out the decisions made by the Assembly. They took care of the city's **administration**, or management.

Pericles

Pericles was a leader in Athens for 30 years. He worked to make Athens the most beautiful city in the world. Pericles said, "Here each individual is interested not only in his own affairs, but in the affairs of the state as well … a man who has no interest in politics … has no business here at all."

— Pericles, c. 450 BCE

Do ⊠ Discuss ⊠ Discover

1. Use an organizer to make notes about the different types of government described on page 72. Include these criteria: type of government, leader or authority, means of gaining power.

The Legal System

The Assembly decided on the laws that the people in Athens had to obey. People who were accused of breaking the law had to go to court.

Trials

A jury was selected from the citizens attending the Assembly. There were no lawyers, but witnesses could give evidence. The person who was charged with the crime and the accuser were each allowed to speak for a certain length of time.

The jury acted as judges and made a decision by voting. Each judge had two bronze disks. The disk for "guilty" had a hole in the knob, and the disk for "innocent" had a solid knob. The disks were dropped into a pot, then counted to decide on guilt or innocence.

Women rarely had a role in trials. They could appear in court to present evidence or try to get a jury to feel pity.

Punishments

Most punishments were fines. The penalty for theft depended on the amount stolen. A slave could be whipped as punishment. The punishment for murder was exile. Athenians believed that the worst thing that could happen was to be made to leave Athens.

Ostracism

Once a year, members of the Assembly of Athens could vote to **ostracize** (banish) criminals or unpopular politicians to get rid of them. Citizens scratched the names of people they wished to banish on broken pieces of pottery called *ostraka*, and dropped them into a pot.

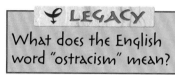

LEGACY
What does the English word "ostracism" mean?

A person who was named by more than 6000 citizens had to leave Athens for ten years.

Group Discussion

A group discussion is a way to extend your learning by sharing and exploring ideas or questions about a topic with other students. It is important to use certain skills to make sure that your group discussion is meaningful.

For an effective discussion, group members need to
- share information and ideas
- explain ideas and give examples
- listen carefully and ask meaningful questions
- stay on topic
- summarize the group's ideas
- form conclusions

Group members help each other in a discussion when they
- show interest by listening to each other's ideas
- respond or add to the ideas of others
- encourage and support one another
- invite each other's ideas
- disagree in agreeable ways

If your group is reporting their ideas following the discussion
- keep point form notes
- review the ideas discussed
- select a person to speak for the group

Do ⊠ Discuss ⊠ Discover

1. In a small group, discuss what democracy means to each of you.

75

Defense and War

The Greek city-states were frequently at war with one another. They fought to gain land or to become more powerful. A city-state that was controlled by another one had to pay an annual tax called tribute. City-states often revolted and refused to pay the tribute, which led to more wars.

City-states sometimes fought with nearby countries, either to defend themselves or to conquer new territory. Each of the Greek city-states had an army. All healthy citizens served in the military at some time in their lives.

Military Service

In Athens when males reached the age of 18 they were given two years of military training to learn how to be soldiers. They were called to serve in the army or navy whenever they were needed. Every year in the spring a list was posted in the agora naming the men expected to serve in the army or navy for that year.

The Greeks were best known for the **hoplites**. The hoplites were very skilled soldiers who fought on foot. They wore helmets, breastplates, and leg guards, and carried shields and spears. Because soldiers had to provide their own armour and weapons, only the wealthier citizens became hoplites. Poorer soldiers served as archers and stone-slingers because the equipment was less expensive.

Only the wealthiest served as cavalry, because horses were expensive to buy and feed.

This bronze hoplite armour would have been smooth and shiny when it was new, over 2000 years ago.

Soldiers hung their armour in trees to thank the gods for helping them survive battles.

Do ⊠ Discuss ⊠ Discover

1. Summarize the information on this page in your notebook. Share your notes with another student. Make changes if necessary.

The Phalanx

In battle the hoplites fought in a square formation (arrangement) called a **phalanx**. This battle strategy made the hoplites very difficult to attack.

Several rows of soldiers stood shoulder to shoulder with their shields up to form a barrier. They moved forward as a block, with their spears extended in front of them. If someone in the front line was injured, another stepped up into his place.

The Athenian Navy

Although Athens had a strong army it was mainly a maritime power. It had a navy of hundreds of warships called triremes to protect Greek harbours and merchant ships from attack. They were also used to attack the boats of other city-states. The navy also had small, fast ships for carrying messages.

The Trireme

A Greek trireme carried a crew of around 200 men who were doing their military service. Up to 170 served as oarsmen who rowed the ship. The rest were armed soldiers on deck.

Triremes were designed to be very fast and easy to steer. They had square sails made of linen. Three rows of oarsmen rowed as a huge team. Two wooden paddles at the stern (back end) were used to steer the trireme.

The oarsmen on triremes rowed in time to music played on a flute.

Each trireme had a bronze battering ram at the front. It sank an enemy ship by smashing a hole in its side.

There was little room on a trireme for any cargo. The three rows of oarsmen took up all of the space under the decks. The ship carried water for the crew, but only enough food for a few days. After a sea battle it had to return home or go to another harbour to get more supplies.

Using Your Learning

Knowledge and Understanding

1. In groups of 3 or 4 discuss why democracy in ancient Greece is called a limited democracy. Decide whether you agree or disagree with this form of democracy. In your notes, write your opinion and explain your reasons.

2. Add the vocabulary words from this chapter to your Vocabulary File. Choose one of the following activities to complete your vocabulary study for ancient Greece.
   - Create a picture dictionary.
   - Make up word games (e.g., riddles, matching words and definitions).
   - Design crossword puzzles or word searches.

Inquiry/Research and Communication Skills

3. The Greeks fought many famous battles. Visit the website http://hometown.aol.com/ TeacherNet to find out more about some of these Greek battles. Describe your findings in your notes.

4. Use an atlas and the map of the Greek colonies you made for the activity on page 71. Find today's names for the lands where the colonies were located. List the modern names in your notes.

5. In resource books or encyclopedias, find a drawing of the phalanx formation. With a partner, discuss why this is an efficient battle strategy.

Application

6. In your notes use a Venn diagram to compare democracy in ancient Athens with democracy in Canada today.

7. The Greek colonists experienced many difficulties. These included
   - a long voyage
   - distance from the protection and culture of Greece
   - threat of attack by non-Greeks living nearby

   Think of other difficulties they would have experienced. Imagine that you are an early Greek colonist, and write a journal entry describing your experiences.

Section I Project

Chapter 6 focused on the political life of the ancient Greeks. With your project group, review the chapter sub-headings. Identify the key information about political life to be illustrated on your History Wall mural. Share the tasks of illustrating it.

Timeline Activity

Refer to the timeline for Greece inside the front cover of the book. Locate the period of ancient Greek history that you have been studying. In your project groups, create a timeline for that period. Use illustrations to make your timeline interesting.

Section I Project

Complete and share your Section I Project. Follow the sequence below:

- Review your Section I notes and activities. Decide on any additional information that you want to add to your History Wall mural.

- Complete your mural by giving it a title. Make label cards for Environment, Economic Life, Social Life, and Political Life, or decorate a cutout of the trireme graphic that includes these labels. Use pieces of string or yarn to connect examples on your mural with these labels for each part of the Model for Learning about a Civilization.

- Decide where you will display your History Wall mural. Some possibilities include the classroom, hallway bulletin board, or the library.

- In your project group, plan how you will share your learning with others. You might explain your mural to other groups in your class. You might invite other classes or adults in your community to view your History Wall and hear about your study of ancient Greece.

- Store your History Wall mural in a safe place so that you can use it again as part of your Section II Project.

SECTION II
ANCIENT CHINA

The civilization of ancient China developed where modern China is today. Ancient China had a written language and a highly organized society. Major public works such as canals and roads were built there. Ancient China developed many types of technology that were unknown anywhere else.

For thousands of years, contact between China and the rest of the world was limited. Some products from China such as silk and fine glazed pottery were traded to other places. Gradually other Chinese inventions became known. These inventions influenced the technology of many other countries.

In this textbook, we will focus on the period of Chinese history from about 220 BCE to about 220 CE. These years were a major period of change and development in China.

Section II Project
PREPARING A HISTORICAL DOCUMENTARY

As you study Section II, use the Model for Learning about Civilizations (pages 4 and 5) to prepare an oral presentation in the form of a documentary about ancient China.

A documentary uses a variety of sources (both pictures and words) and presents factual information about a topic. Use the model as a guide in collecting key information about the environment and economic, social, and political life in ancient China.

Prepare for your project by forming groups of 4 or 5. As you study Section II, collect or create artifacts, maps, illustrations, photos, diagrams, charts, and graphs to show key information about ancient China. Prepare skits and demonstrations as part of your final oral presentation.

Throughout Section II, you will be given reminders and suggestions for completing your Historical Documentary.

Locating Ancient China

Ancient China was located where modern China is found today, in the southeastern part of the continent of Asia. China is a huge and varied country of hills, plains, mountains, and deserts.

The earliest Chinese civilization developed on the fertile plains around the Huang He (Yellow River) and the Chang Jiang (Yangtze River).

This textbook will look at two periods of Chinese history: the Qin (pronounced *chin*) **dynasty** and the Han dynasty. Dynasties are historical periods named after the ruling family of the time.

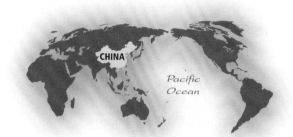

**Qin Dynasty
(221BCE–206 BCE)**

- ⬛ Area of Qin dynasty
- ---- Extent of Great Wall
- ⬜ China today

**Han Dynasty
(202 BCE–220 CE)**

- ⬛ Area of Han dynasty
- ---- Extent of Great Wall
- ⬜ China today

China Today

China today is the third largest country in the world. Canada is the second largest. China today includes more land to the northwest and the northeast than in ancient times.

The region of Hong Kong returned to Chinese control in 1997 after 99 years as a colony of Great Britain. The island of Taiwan has governed itself as a separate country since 1949. However, the government of the People's Republic of China considers it to be a province of China.

Beijing is the capital of modern China.

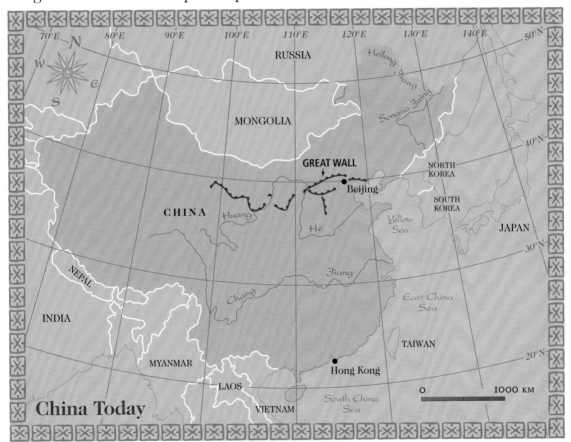

China Today

Do ⌗ Discuss ⌗ Discover

1. On an outline map of modern China, locate and label the places and bodies of water shown on the map above.

   a) Use one colour to indicate the boundary of ancient China under the Qin dynasty, shown on page 82.

   b) With a second colour, show the expansion under the Han dynasty.(See page 82.)

   c) Include a title, legend, and compass rose on your map.

   d) Under your map, write a brief description of ancient China, including its location. Put your map in your notebook.

economic life · social life · political life

culture

the environment

Chapter 7
The Environment

The ancient Chinese civilization developed in the green hills, river valleys, and plains of the eastern part of China today. China is a huge country made up of many environmental regions. It contains some of the world's most fertile plains, driest deserts, and highest mountains.

Focus on Learning

In this chapter you will learn about
- reading contour lines
- landforms and bodies of water found in ancient China
- climate and vegetation of ancient China
- animal life and natural resources of ancient China

Vocabulary

contour line	sediment
relief map	monsoon
plateau	naturalize
gorge	jade

Reading Contour Lines

Contour lines connect points on a map that have the same elevation. That means that each point along a contour line is the same height above sea level.

Contour lines are one way to create a map that shows the shapes of landforms. Contour maps are a type of **relief map**.

Contours show what you would see if landforms were sliced across horizontally and the edges of the slices traced. The contour lines on a map are usually drawn at regular intervals; for example, at every 50 metres of elevation.

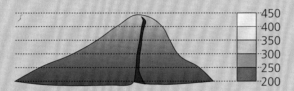

The peak of the highest mountain in a range may be marked and the actual elevation shown.

In places where the contour lines are close together, they represent a steep slope. In places where they are far apart, the slope is shallow. The diagram in the upper right-hand corner shows this.

Some relief maps use both contours and colour to indicate the three-dimensional surface of landforms. A legend shows the colour of each interval. The map of China on the next page uses this method.

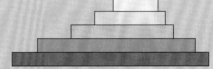

Do ⊠ Discuss ⊠ Discover

1. Work in a small group to create a three-dimensional model of the hill on this page.

   a) Copy each contour in the example onto thick corrugated cardboard.

   b) Cut out each piece and glue the layers together in sequence. Follow the diagram above.

   c) With a felt pen, mark the location of the highest elevation.

Landforms

The ancient Chinese culture first developed among hills, valleys, and rich fertile plains.

There are huge mountain ranges, high-elevation flat areas called **plateaus,** and deserts to the west. These influenced the development of ancient China. They formed a barrier that made contact between the Chinese and other civilizations to the west difficult.

The hills and plains of China were home to large farming communities.

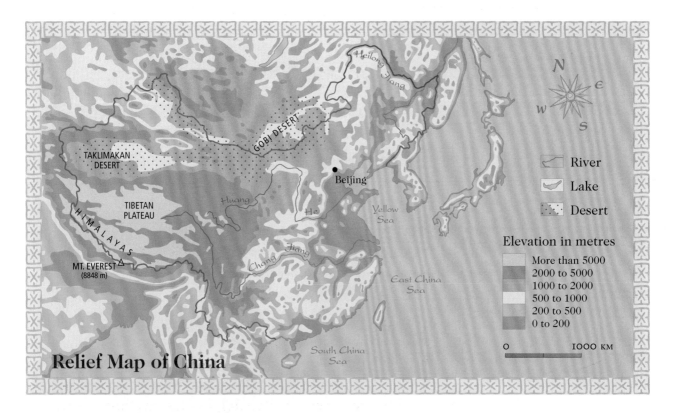

Relief Map of China

River

Lake

Desert

Elevation in metres

More than 5000
2000 to 5000
1000 to 2000
500 to 1000
200 to 500
0 to 200

0   1000 KM

High mountains and deserts made travel between ancient China and other places difficult.

Do ⊠ Discuss ⊠ Discover

1. Discuss the following with a partner.

a) What is the lowest elevation in modern China? What is the highest elevation? What is the range in elevation from lowest to highest?

b) Make predictions about how elevation may affect climate and vegetation.

Bodies of Water

Two of the world's longest rivers are found in China. The Huang He (Yellow River) and Chang Jiang (Yangtze River) begin high in the mountains in the west. They flow eastward through deep, steep-sided mountain **gorges**. They cross the broad plains to the sea.

Many warm beaches of the South China Sea are suitable for swimming.

The Chang Jiang flows across central China to the East China Sea. Many large shallow lakes are found near the Chang Jiang.

The Chang Jiang begins in the mountains.

The Huang He gets its name from the yellowish **sediment** in it. These particles of sand and earth in the water originated as dust blown from the Gobi Desert. It flows into the Yellow Sea.

China's coastline is about 6500 km long. The Yellow Sea has shallow coastal waters with many good fishing grounds. There are many inlets and islands along the southern coast.

Fertile Floods

Snow melting in the western mountains and heavy winter rains cause rivers in China to flood. Large rivers erode their channels. They cut gorges and carry away particles of rock and soil. Sometimes a river cuts a new channel and abandons the old riverbed.

Rivers flatten out and slow down when they leave the mountains and enter an area of plains. The particles of soil carried by the river are left behind in the riverbed or on the flood plain. Tonnes of sediment are added to the rich earth of the plains each year.

Floods on the Huang He and Chang Jiang have caused millions of deaths throughout history.

Yellowish sediment is carried in the waters of the Huang He.

Do ⊠ Discuss ⊠ Discover

1. In groups, discuss ways that parts of an environment influence one another. Predict two ways that this interrelationship would affect the culture of ancient China.

2. Create a title page in your notebook for Section II. Show the environment of China.

Climate

The climate of China has changed little since ancient times. Different regions of modern China have different climates. Latitude, elevation, nearness to large bodies of water, and winds all affect the climate.

In central and southeastern China, it is hot and wet in summer and somewhat cooler and drier in winter. Southern coastal areas stay warm and humid most of the year. The highlands of the west and north are cold in winter and fairly cool in summer.

Most of China has a dry season in winter and a wetter season in summer. In winter, cold dry **monsoon** winds blow from the northwest. Monsoon winds change direction in different seasons. In summer, hot wet monsoon winds blow from the southeast. These carry warm wet air from the sea.

Average January Temperature

Average temperature (° Celsius)

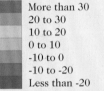

More than 30
20 to 30
10 to 20
0 to 10
-10 to 0
-10 to -20
Less than -20

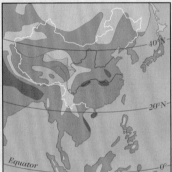

Average July Temperature

Coastal areas have typhoons in late summer. These high winds can do terrible damage along the coasts, as hurricanes do in North America.

Average Winter Precipitation

Average monthly precipitation (mm)

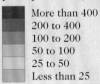

More than 400
200 to 400
100 to 200
50 to 100
25 to 50
Less than 25

Average Summer Precipitation

Do ⊠ Discuss ⊠ Discover

1. Compare the latitudes of ancient China and ancient Greece (see page 14). Discuss the effect of latitude on climate in each area.

2. Compare the elevation of western China and eastern China, and discuss how this might affect climate.

3. In one-sentence summaries, describe the trends shown in each set of weather maps on this page.

Vegetation

Thousands of kinds of plants are native to China. However, it is difficult to be sure what grew in different regions before the land was farmed. Some parts of modern China have been farmed for over 7000 years.

The vegetation in the southeast where it is warm and wet is very different from the colder, drier regions to the north and west.

Lychee fruit (shown above), apricots, peaches, apples, oranges, and tangerines all grew in ancient China.

Rhododendrons (shown above), rice, sugar cane, rapeseed, tea, cotton, and wheat have grown in China for thousands of years.

Forests of cypress, pine, and bamboo (shown above) grow in hilly or mountainous places where farming is not possible.

Other trees include rubber trees (shown above), mulberry, boxwood, palm, oak, maple, birch, and banyan.

Animal Life

The huge area that is China today has more than 2000 native species of animals. In ancient China, animals, birds, and fish were hunted, raised for food, and kept as pets.

Many animals that came from China are now found in other parts of the world. Many are in zoos. Some, like the ring-necked pheasant, were introduced into other environments and have naturalized.

Greater and lesser panda bears, elephants, monkeys, goats, white-lipped deer, camels, water buffalo, donkeys, tigers, and black bears are just a few Chinese animals.

Carp (shown above), dogfish, goldfish, minnow, and sucker were found in ancient China. Fish were raised in fishponds as well as caught in seas, rivers, and lakes.

Panda bears live on bamboo. The bears' habitat is being reduced as bamboo forests are cut down.

Natural Resources

Mineral resources in China that were mined in ancient times included coal, iron ore, tin, lead, copper, gold, and salt. Clay used to make pottery and tiles was mined from clay pits.

Various kinds of building stone and **jade** were quarried in ancient China. Jade is a type of hard, beautiful stone. It can be carved to make jewellery and objects of art, like the jade dog on the right.

Rich fertile soil grew crops that met people's needs and provided surplus for trade. Forests of pine and bamboo provided wood for building. Many kinds of birds, animals, and fish were sources of food.

Tigers are now found mainly in nature preserves where they are protected from hunters.

Using Your Learning

Knowledge and Understanding

1. Carefully review the illustration on page 84. In your notes, list all the details about the environment of ancient China that you can find in the picture. Explain what each item on your list tells you about the environment of China.

2. Use a chart like the one shown below to predict how the environment may have influenced the way that the ancient Chinese culture developed.

Environment	Description	Influences
Land		
Bodies of Water		
Climate		
Vegetation		
Animal Life		
Natural Resources		

EXAMPLE

3. Begin a new Vocabulary File for your study of ancient China. Use a file box with alphabetical index cards (or create a computer file) to store your vocabulary words. Give each word a definition and sketch a visual reminder of the word. File your words alphabetically.

Inquiry/Research and Communication Skills

4. Take a tour of China today. Go to the library or visit websites such as http://members.tripod.de/yoshikeller/china/index.htm, www.travelchinaguide.com/picture/index.htm, or www.chinavista.com/travel/virtualtours.html to find photos of Chinese landscapes. Design a travel brochure for China to include in your notes.

Application

5. Read the maps showing the average temperatures and amounts of precipitation for China on page 88. Re-read the charts for Greece on page 14. Compare winter and summer seasons in China and Greece on a graphic organizer.

6. With a partner, discuss how information about the environment of China can help you make predictions about what you will learn about the economic life of ancient China in the next chapter.

Section II Project

Review the sub-headings in this chapter and your notes to recall what you have learned about the environment of ancient China. Begin preparation for your Historical Documentary. Create or collect materials such as maps, photos, illustrations, video clips, or written accounts that demonstrate this environment. In your group, share the tasks involved in preparing this part of your presentation. Decide on an appropriate method of filing and storing the materials you prepare for this part of your documentary.

economic life · social life · political life · culture · the environment

Chapter 8
Meeting Basic Needs

China's many natural resources enabled people to meet their basic needs from their environment. Food, homes, and clothing all came from local resources and products. Herbal medicines and other methods were used to prevent illness and to treat health conditions.

Focus on Learning

In this chapter you will learn about
- how the environment enabled the ancient Chinese to meet their basic needs
- the foods they ate and how these foods were obtained
- ancient Chinese homes
- the clothing of the ancient Chinese
- healthcare in ancient China

Vocabulary

millet
harmony
social class

hemp
herbalist
acupuncture

Food

Foods grown in China varied somewhat, depending on the region. **Millet** was a staple in the north where the climate was drier and cooler. Millet is a cereal grass with numerous small round grains. Wheat was also grown in the north. Various kinds of noodles, buns, pancakes, and dumplings were made from flour. Rice was a staple for people living in the hotter, wetter parts of southern China. It was also eaten in other regions.

Chinese people ate many fruits and vegetables. Some examples are lychees, waterchestnuts, snow peas, soybeans, melons, and Chinese cabbage.

1. ginger
2. soybeans
3. mung beans
4. *gai lan*
5. *bok choy*
6. dried squid
7. Chinese radish
8. oranges
9. snow peas
10. garlic
11. wheat
12. millet
13. rice
14. dried mushrooms
15. tea

Most people's diets included some fish or a little meat such as chicken. Rural villages often had a fishpond where they raised fish by aquaculture. Wealthier people ate more meat and had more variety in their diet.

A variety of herbs and spices were used to create flavours that were sweet, sour, hot, or salty. Cinnamon, ginger, garlic, salt, sugar, honey, and soy sauce were used to season foods. Foods such as mushrooms and seafood were often dried to preserve them. Drying kept them from spoiling. They were stored to use later in cooking.

Drinks

The ancient Chinese were the first tea drinkers. People also drank water mixed with honey, ginger, and fruit juices.

Water was obtained from rivers, canals, lakes, or wells. In winter, people living in colder regions cut ice from the rivers and lakes. They stored it in earth mounds to keep it frozen for use in the summer.

The Art of Cooking

Food was more than a necessity of life for the ancient Chinese. Cooking was considered to be an art, and food was carefully prepared and served. Presentation in attractive dishes was important.

Wealthier people ate many kinds of meat, fish, and vegetables, which they seasoned with herbs and spices. Their food was boiled, steamed in bamboo containers, fried in a shallow pan called a *wok*, or sometimes roasted. Their dishes were made of fine pottery or wood covered with lacquer (a kind of varnish).

To save on fuel, cooks cut food into bite-sized pieces so it cooked more quickly. This also made it easy to serve and eat.

Eating

Meals were served in the morning, at noon, and in the evening. Usually men and boys over seven ate first. When their meal was completed, the women and other children ate together.

Pairs of wooden sticks called chopsticks were used for eating. Food was served in small bowls, which could be held close to the mouth.

The poor had simpler meals. They usually ate foods like beans, grains, vegetables, and sometimes a little meat or fish. Most of their food was steamed over boiling water. Their cooking utensils were simple, and they ate from rough wooden or pottery dishes.

Do ⊠ Discuss ⊠ Discover

1. In your notebook, sketch and label four foods eaten by the ancient Chinese.

2. In a paragraph, describe how the environment of ancient China helped provide for the people's basic need for food. Include ways that what they ate was restricted by what their environment produced.

Let's Have Chinese Food!

Going out for Chinese food or ordering take-out food is a familiar part of life today.

During the 1800s and 1900s, hundreds of thousands of Chinese men and a few women were hired to be workers in other parts of the world. These workers hoped to earn money to send back to their villages in China.

About 15 000 Chinese workers came to Canada to work on building the railroad in the late 1800s. The work was hard and dangerous and quite a few workers died. Some eventually returned to China, but others stayed in Canada. Many other Chinese people have immigrated to Canada since then.

Chinese people and their descendents have preserved some of their traditional culture, such as favourite foods and celebrations. Many of these foods have become popular and are eaten by most Canadians.

Today, rice is a common staple in most Canadian homes. Soy sauce is used as a flavouring, and tofu is available in many forms. Vegetables such as bok choy (Chinese cabbage) and

The Chinese were using chopsticks for eating when people in most of the world were still using their hands.

gai lan (Chinese greens), as well as fresh or tinned lychee, can be bought in many grocery stores.

But if you don't feel like cooking, then how about getting take-out?

Using Chopsticks

Hold one chopstick between the thumb and the fourth finger. This one does not move.

Hold the other chopstick with your thumb and first two fingers. This one moves.

Grasp pieces of food between the two ends, or pick up rice with a scooping motion.

Homes

People of ancient China built their homes to be in **harmony** with the natural world. They made careful choices about design and materials to create balance and order. Homes were built from materials from the environment, such as wood, bamboo, brick, and tile. They were square or rectangular and carefully placed with respect to the four directions.

Roofs had upturned corners. The ancient Chinese believed that evil spirits travelled in straight lines and the upturned corners kept them away.

Large Traditional Homes

During the Han dynasty, homes of wealthy families were large, with many rooms and fireplaces. They were comfortable and well-constructed. Homes were built around a central courtyard. They often had a wall around the outside.

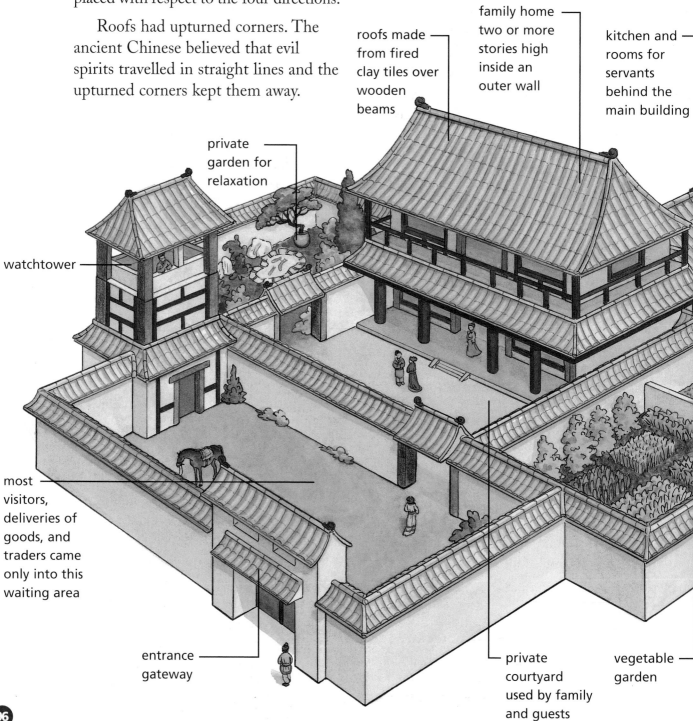

roofs made from fired clay tiles over wooden beams

family home two or more stories high inside an outer wall

kitchen and rooms for servants behind the main building

private garden for relaxation

watchtower

most visitors, deliveries of goods, and traders came only into this waiting area

entrance gateway

private courtyard used by family and guests

vegetable garden

Furniture

Adults and children slept on mats made from rushes or padded material, with wooden headrests rather than pillows. In northern China, people slept on raised platforms that were heated underneath.

Wealthier people had elaborately carved tables and storage chests. Their walls were plastered and painted with floral designs. Some walls displayed paintings or bronze mirrors.

The top of this bronze lamp held oil, which was burned for light.

Rooms were furnished with low tables and cupboards made of bamboo or wood.

Other Types of Homes

Some people lived in simple wood-framed one-room huts. The roofs were thatched and the walls made of a mixture of mud or plaster and twigs.

Often several farming families lived in a large shared house and worked in their fields together. The courtyard of the farmhouse was used for threshing and drying grain and growing vegetables. Barns and other buildings surrounded the farmhouse. Storage rooms were built on stilts. This protected the grain and other foods from rats and dampness.

In the cities, poorer families lived in crowded conditions. Often several families lived together in multi-storey homes. There was usually a shop or business on the ground floor.

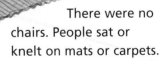

There were no chairs. People sat or knelt on mats or carpets.

Decorated screens, beautiful fabric wall hangings, and woollen carpets were found in many large homes.

Do ⊠ Discuss ⊠ Discover

1. In groups of three, discuss ways that the Chinese homes were influenced by their environment.
2. In your notebook, make notes on Chinese homes using a web. Remember to include notes for information provided in illustrations and captions, as well as the text.

Clothing

In China, a person's clothing showed his or her **social class** and importance. A person's position in relation to the other groups in a culture was very important in ancient China. There were rules and expectations about how people from different social classes should behave. This included what they were allowed to wear.

Women from higher classes wore long flowing robes, dresses, or skirts and jackets made of silk. They wore earrings, and they particularly liked jewelled hair ornaments. They powdered their faces and wore rouge to colour their cheeks.

Hats indicated a person's class or occupation. Men would not be seen in public without a hat.

Clothing for the poor was simple. Both men and women wore shirts and pants made of **hemp**, plant fibres woven into a rough fabric. Some wore straw sandals or wooden clogs on their feet, but many went barefoot. In winter, poor people stuffed their clothes with straw or cloth to keep themselves warm.

Only the emperor was allowed to wear a certain shade of yellow.

Men from the higher classes wore belted robes with long wide sleeves lined with silk. In winter, they wore warm fur coats, made of squirrel or fox skins, and leather slippers. They wore leather slippers or boots, or shoes lined with silk.

Wealthy people or people from the higher classes wore jewellery made of jade, gold, silver, or brass. Others wore jewellery made from copper or iron.

Do ▧ Discuss ▧ Discover

1. Skim through Section II and look at the hats that men are wearing. Sketch examples of three different hats in your notes. Explain what you think each hat tells about the person and his position.

2. Examine the pictures of the clothing worn by the wealthy people and the poor people. Create a comparison chart to show differences and similarities.

Silk

Fabrics used by wealthy and upper-class people were woven in coloured patterns or decorated with embroidery.

People from the higher classes and the Emperor's family always wore silk. Chinese women raised silkworms and produced beautiful silk fabric.

Silkworms eat only the leaves of mulberry trees. The larva or caterpillar of the silk moth was fed on the mulberry leaves for several months. Then it spun a cocoon of raw silk around itself.

To harvest the silk, women soaked the cocoons in water. Then they carefully unwound the cocoons and rewound the thin fibres onto spools. The fibres were twisted together to make heavier thread and the thread woven into fabric. The silk was usually dyed beautiful, rich colours.

Clothing was often decorated with mythical animals and symbols to protect the wearer from harm and bring good fortune. The peony in the piece of embroidery on the left was a symbol of spring. It was known as the "king of flowers."

Health

The ancient Chinese believed that everything in nature must be in harmony. Illness was the result of the forces within the body being out of balance. They believed that exercise and proper food brought good health. They developed advanced methods of preventing and treating sickness.

Herbalists used a variety of plants and products from the environment to treat conditions like pain, fever, or colds. To destroy germs, the ancient Chinese burned a chemical to produce a poisonous smoke. They did this to prevent the spread of disease.

Either men or women could be doctors. They used herbal treatments, **acupuncture**, and moxibustion to treat illnesses.

Sharp, thin acupuncture needles were used to treat different conditions. The needles stimulated forces in the body or blocked pain. Doctors memorized charts of hundreds of places on the body as part of their training.

Moxibustion was used to treat long-lasting pain. Dried leaves of the moxa plant were applied to various parts of the body. The leaves were set on fire and the ashes rubbed into the blisters.

Herbal Treatments	
Health Condition	**Treatment**
rheumatism, broken bones	teasel root
dizziness	mulberries
stiffness, lower back pain	chain fern bark
fatigue, lack of appetite	Chinese yam
high blood pressure, rheumatism	mulberry wood
cold, headache, measles	bugbane rhizome (a plant root)
intestinal problems	senna leaf
eyesight problems, diabetes	wolfberry

♀ LEGACY

Forms of acupuncture and moxibustion are still used today in China. Acupuncture is used to treat conditions such as asthma, stomach ulcers, migraines, and arthritis. Acupuncture treatments are now used in Canada and in other countries.

Using Your Learning

Knowledge and Understanding

1. Make a web in your notes like the one shown below. Complete the web to show how the ancient Chinese met their basic needs.

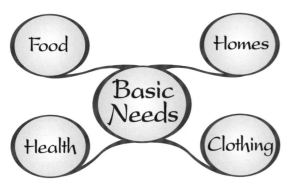

2. Add definitions and sketches to your Vocabulary File for the vocabulary words in this chapter.

Inquiry/Research and Communication Skills

3. Locate a menu from a local Chinese restaurant that describes the food you can order. Compare local Chinese food with the food eaten by the ancient Chinese. Describe the similarities and differences in your notes.

4. Use encyclopedias, library resource books, or the Internet to find out more about the mulberry tree. Make a feature page for your notes illustrating the tree and its uses.

Application

5. Make a collection of small samples of different kinds of fabrics. Sort these samples and classify them according to whether they would have been used by the ancient Chinese or not. Make a poster showing your information in chart form. Label each sample and paste it in the appropriate category.

6. Use the information and illustrations on pages 96 and 97 to draw a floor plan of an imaginary ancient Chinese home. Include labels for all of the parts of the home.

economic life
social life
political life
culture
the environment

Chapter 9
Work and Trade

Work and trade are an important part of economic life. People in ancient China worked hard to provide for the basic needs of the large population. Although many people were poor, the Chinese empire was wealthy. Many government services were provided, including a large army. Trade brought wealth and imported products.

Focus on Learning

In this chapter you will learn about
• the economic life in ancient China
• farming, fishing, and mining
• how to make an oral presentation
• how artisans and merchants contributed to meeting basic needs
• trading in ancient China

Vocabulary

peasants
conscription
sampan

smelting
lacquerware
scribe

Economic Life in Ancient China

Economic life in ancient China was based on farming. Most of the people were **peasant** farmers, but only a few owned their small plots of land.

Most peasants worked and lived on the large estates of wealthy nobles as tenant farmers. They paid large rents for the plots of land they farmed. The poorest peasants were labourers who earned a wage by working for others. Farmers grew food for themselves, the army, and people in the cities.

People in the cities worked as craftspeople, in professions, business, and trade. People in professions included public (government) officials, teachers, and doctors.

Many people worked in services, such as doing repairs, cleaning, and providing care. Wealthy people had many paid household servants.

Most women worked in the home. They often added to the family income by raising silkworms, making products such as sandals for sale, or keeping chickens. Some women ran small shops or worked as doctors or herbalists.

Public Works

The people of ancient China benefited from public works that the government organized. Canals and roads were built for public transportation and communication. Public works were paid for by everyone through taxes and labour.

Conscription

Each year, each adult male (except nobles and public officials) had to do one month of work for the government. This was part of their taxes and was unpaid. Being called up to do government service, either as a soldier or a worker, is called **conscription**.

Poor people worked on road building and canal digging projects. Others had jobs working in the iron or salt industries. These industries were so important that they were controlled by the government. Prisoners were forced to work on government projects.

Men in ancient China were also conscripted to spend two years in the army at some time in their adult life. China had a very long border that had to be defended against invaders all the time.

Farming

Farmers in the north of China grew millet and wheat for flour and hemp for its fibres. In the south and central part of China, the major crop was rice.

In hilly country, farmers created terraces to increase the amount of farmland. Terraces also reduced erosion of the hillsides during the heavy monsoon rains.

Chinese farmers also grew fruit trees and many kinds of vegetables. They kept dogs, pigs, sheep, and chickens.

Farm families were able to sell or trade some of their surplus produce. This earned extra money for clothing, salt, and other necessities. Some also grew mulberry trees for raising silkworms. They also gathered herbs and products such as mushrooms from the environment to sell at the markets.

Hunters living in farming communities supplied wealthy people with meat from wild birds, deer, and other animals. They used falcons (birds of prey), hounds, and bows and arrows for hunting.

Farming Technology

Most farm families weeded crops by hand with hoes, carried water to their crops in buckets, and ground grain with simple mills. Wealthier farmers had animals such as oxen or buffalo to pull their ploughs. Farmers who could afford them used machines such as wheelbarrows to make their work easier.

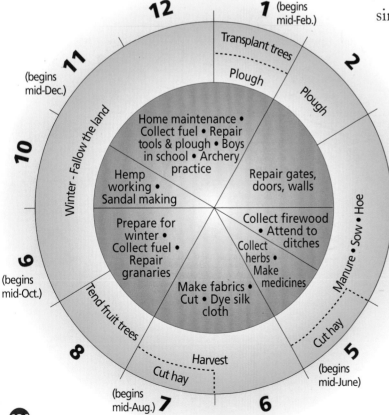

Around 100 CE, a calendar was developed by the government to help farmers schedule their activities. Each month began with the new moon. (This is a simplified version of the calendar. Every few years there were 13 months in the year.)

Growing Rice

Rice was a staple food in ancient China. Small rice plants called seedlings were transplanted by hand into the soft mud of flooded fields called rice paddies. Rice needs very wet conditions to grow, so the fields were kept flooded until the plants matured.

The farmers of ancient China hoed and weeded the rice plants as they grew. Children frightened birds away from the grain with noisemakers. Farmers often slept in the fields to guard the crop from thieves.

The ripe plants were pulled up or cut with a hand sickle. A flail was used to thresh the seeds from the plant heads. The rice straw was gathered and used for making thatch, woven mats, and sandals.

The machine in this illustration raised water to flood the field above.

Fishing

The Chinese fished in the seas along the coastline, in rivers, lakes, and canals. Flooded rice paddies were sometimes stocked with fish.

Fishers used rod and line from shore, a raft, or a small flat-bottomed boat called a **sampan**. Sometimes they lured fish to the surface at night with a lamp.

A diving bird called a cormorant was trained to scoop fish from the water. The cormorant was attached to the raft or sampan by a long cord. It had a ring around its neck so it couldn't swallow the fish.

The fishing reel was invented in China. It was adapted from the design of a machine used in warfare.

Do ✕ Discuss ✕ Discover

1. Discuss the following with a partner:
   a) Why was farming important to the ancient Chinese economy?
   b) Do you think cormorant fishing was an effective way of fishing? Why or why not?

Make a Sampan

You will need

- ruler
- glue
- paintbrush
- string

- pencil
- light cardboard (20 cm x 28 cm)
- 4 bamboo barbecue skewers
- pale yellow paper (20 cm x 28 cm)

- masking tape
- brown paint

1. Measure and draw sampan pieces onto card. Draw two each of runner (D) and platform (E).

2. Cut out all pieces of card. Score lightly along all fold (dotted) lines, including tabs. Bend up tabs on all pieces.

3. Fold up side pieces (A), bottom pieces (B), and end pieces (C) to form the sampan.

4. Glue tabs on B and C to sides (A). Use masking tape to hold the pieces while the glue dries.

5. Glue runners (D) along top edges of sides of the boat. They should stick out 1.5 cm from the ends.

6. At each end of sampan, glue platform pieces (E) to tabs marked * on A and C.

7. Cut 16 cm pieces from two barbecue skewers. Bend to form arches 6 cm high. Cut two skewers into 7 cm crosspieces. Glue and tie crosspieces to arches to make roof frame.

8. Paint boat and allow to dry. Draw lines on the sides to represent boards.

9. Fold strips of yellow paper (F) to make roof matting. Glue strips to frame. When completely dry, place roof into boat.

F x24 (paper)
7 cm
1 cm

3.5 cm

E x2 (card)
5 cm

D x2 (card)
5 mm
5 mm

5 mm
5 mm

5 mm
7 cm
A
1.5 cm
7 cm
5 mm

*C
B
7 cm
(card)
8 cm
3.5 cm
B
7 cm
C*

7 cm
A
1.5 cm
7 cm

5 mm
5 mm

Mining

Archaeologists have found elaborate bronze containers in tombs in China that are more than 3500 years old. Bronze is made from a mixture of metals, mainly copper and tin. Both copper and tin were mined in China in earliest times.

Iron was a harder metal than bronze. It was a stronger metal for making tools and weapons. The ancient Chinese **smelted** iron ore at very high heats to remove the metal from the ore. They were the first people to make cast iron. They added carbon to the liquid metal, then poured the metal into a mold.

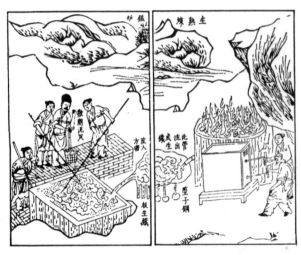

In the ancient Chinese drawing above, the workers on the right are forcing air into the round furnace with a bellows machine. The molten iron flows into a tank. The ironworkers on the left mix it with other substances to make it stronger.

Jade was mined in China. It was used to carve beautiful works of art such as sculptures or vases and to make precious jewellery.

The ancient Chinese developed iron drills to mine for salt underground. Salt was essential for preserving food. Previously, seawater had been the only source of salt, so people who lived far from the ocean had to obtain salt through trade.

The crosspiece on the tower acted as a pulley. This helped workers raise and lower buckets into the salt mine.

A fine clay called kaolin and other types of clay were mined from clay pits.

Do ⊠ Discuss ⊠ Discover

1. Imagine that you are an iron smelter worker. Describe in writing what your work is like, or act it out with a partner.

2. Discuss why salt was so valuable to the ancient Chinese. Name two foods that can be preserved using salt.

Making an Oral Presentation

When you make an oral presentation, you give a talk to an audience about a topic that you have learned about. The process has four parts:

Prepare for your presentation:
- Select your topic and research your material.
- Develop your ideas in a logical manner (prepare cue cards as reminders).
- Plan an interesting opening and a logical conclusion.
- Arrange for props or audio-visual materials you wish to use.
- Rehearse your presentation.

During your presentation:
- Maintain eye contact with your audience and use good posture.
- Speak at a reasonable pace and volume.
- Use your voice to emphasize important ideas.
- Use hand gestures and facial expressions that are natural and relaxed.
- Use props or audio-visual materials smoothly.

Prepare for questions about your topic:
- Think about why your topic is important.
- How does it relate to other things or ideas?
- Why does it interest you?
- How can your information be used?

Ask for feedback

After your presentation, your teacher or your audience can give you feedback. Ask which parts of your presentation were effective and which parts you still need to practise.

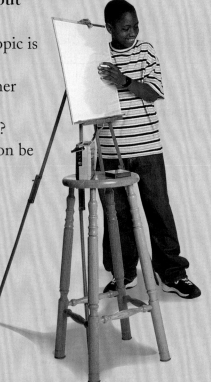

Do ▧ Discuss ▧ Discover

1. Imagine that you are a person living in China during the Qin or Han dynasty. Decide who you will be, then prepare a three-minute oral presentation about your life and your work for the class.

Artisans and Craftspeople

Artisans and craftspeople of ancient China created objects and artwork with attention to detail and style. Objects used in ceremonies often had intricate decoration on their surfaces. Everyday, practical objects were made in simple graceful styles by skilled men and women. Objects were often beautifully decorated with symbols for protection and luck.

This set of bells could be played by a musician, who struck the bells with a drumstick.

The homes of wealthy people often had painted decoration or carvings on roof beams, roof corners, and walls. Furniture was carefully made and intricately carved.

Ancient Chinese metalworkers used clay moulds to cast bronze and iron. They made ceremonial pots, statues, bells, mirrors, tools, and weapons.

This ceremonial axehead was cast from bronze.

Factories

The government set up factories where craftspeople worked together to mass-produce farming tools and weapons. Factories were also established for making silk and producing **lacquerware**. Lacquerware dishes and objects were covered with a kind of varnish that made them water resistant and strong (see page 110).

Everything used by the emperor, his family, and the members of the court had to be the finest quality possible. Nothing unattractive, damaged, or worn out was permitted. Thousands of craftspeople made their livings serving these needs and wants.

Fine pottery like this covered container often had coloured glazes.

Lacquerware

Chinese artisans developed a method of giving wood, cloth, or bamboo articles a beautiful protective finish with lacquer. Dishes covered with many layers of lacquer could withstand heat and water. Dishes, furniture, boxes, and many other decorative items were made using this method.

A pair of these ear-shaped lacquer cups snapped together to form a box for carrying food.

Lacquer was the first type of plastic. It came from the sap of a type of sumac tree that grows in China. The sap is naturally grey. Artisans tinted it black, bright red, gold, green, yellow, and brown to make it more colourful.

Lacquerware objects were often carved or painted with different colours of lacquer. Scenes from nature were popular. Materials such as mother-of-pearl from shells might be set into the surface. Sometimes gold was painted onto part of the design. Many different artisans might work on a piece that was very special.

↯ LEGACY

Furniture, dishes, and decorative items that use Chinese styles, patterns, and artistic techniques have been popular in the rest of the world since they first became known.

Merchants and Business People

Merchants and business people in ancient China bought products and produce from farmers, traders, and craftspeople. Then they sold or traded the goods to people who wanted or needed them. Products from a wide area were sold in the cities of ancient China. The canal and road system was built as public works to make transportation and trade more efficient.

Although they were often wealthy, merchants were considered to be in a very low social class. They weren't respected by either the higher class Chinese or the peasants (farmers and rural workers). Great value was placed on producing a product from your work. Merchants' wealth came from exchanging goods that they did not produce themselves. However, business and trade were important to the Chinese economy, so merchants were tolerated.

The government taxed the merchants heavily to prevent them from making too much money or becoming too powerful. Important industries were usually controlled by the government, not merchants. These included the iron, salt, and coin-making industries.

Numeric Symbols					
Arabic	Ancient Chinese	Modern Chinese	Arabic	Ancient Chinese	Modern Chinese
1	I	一	20	=	二十
2	II	二	30	≡	三十
3	III	三	40	≣	四十
4	IIII	四	50	≣	五十
5	IIIII	五	60	⊥	六十
6	T	六	70	⊥	七十
7	Π	七	80	⊥	八十
8	Ⲧ	八	90	≙	九十
9	Ⲧ	九	100	I	一百
10	—	十			

Merchants used many kinds of calculations in their business records. Builders and scientists also used the Chinese number system.

Coins called "cash" were introduced by the First Emperor and used for 2000 years in China. They could be strung on a cord and attached to a belt.

Do ⊠ Discuss ⊠ Discover

1. Use ancient Chinese numbers to write the day, month, and year that you were born. Is it easier or more difficult for you to write numbers this way? Explain your reasoning.

2. Use ancient Chinese numbers to make two math problems. Exchange with a friend and try to solve each other's problems.

The Marketplace

The market in a Chinese city opened at noon each day with the beating of drums. It was a busy place, crowded with people buying and selling a wide variety of items. The muddy streets were jammed with carts and people carrying baskets and driving animals.

Farmers brought their produce to market to sell. Merchants and craftspeople set up stalls to display their wares. Delicious aromas from cooking food filled the air.

Storytellers, jugglers, and musicians provided free entertainment. **Scribes** (letter writers), fortune-tellers, and barbers offered their services for people to hire.

Trade

Trade within the Chinese empire was important because it was so large. Goods were exchanged between different regions of China. Grain, vegetables, fruit, meat, fabric, silk, weapons, and pottery were traded.

In earliest times, there was little reason to trade outside China. However, invading warriors from central Asia had swift horses, which made them dangerous enemies. Horses were scarce in China and expensive to buy and feed. The Chinese wanted bigger, faster horses to strengthen their army. Eventually, this led to overland trade with other countries.

The Silk Road

The countries in central Asia and the Mediterranean region were eager to trade with China. They particularly wanted silk and beautiful crafts and works of art. An overland trade route between Asia and Europe developed. China's trading partners put such a high value on Chinese silk that the route was called the Silk Road.

The Silk Road wound its way 11 000 km across Asia through rugged mountains and harsh deserts. It ran from the ancient Chinese capital of Chang'an (now called Xian) to the shores of the Mediterranean Sea.

Camels

Trading caravans along the Silk Road used camels because of the harsh conditions. Asian camels have two large humps on their backs where they store large amounts of water. This helps them survive for long periods without drinking.

Camels' large two-toed feet spread wide to keep them from sinking into the sand. Camels can sense changes in the weather that humans cannot detect. Camels in a caravan would stop, kneel down, and refuse to move if they sensed a storm coming. This often saved lives.

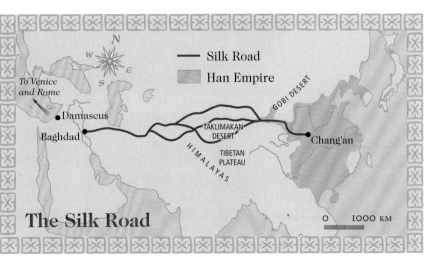

The Silk Road

— Silk Road

Han Empire

To Venice and Rome

Damascus

Baghdad

HIMALAYAS

TAKLIMAKAN DESERT

TIBETAN PLATEAU

GOBI DESERT

Chang'an

0   1000 KM

Sea-going Trade

Chinese sea traders travelled all around the Asian seas. They used sailing ships called junks that could carry large loads of fish or trade goods.

The ancient Chinese developed a heavy steering oar called a rudder. This device made it possible to build and sail very large boats long before ships of that size were built in other countries.

Exports	Imports
silk	horses
jade	silver
lacquerware	gold
works of art	precious stones
rice	glass
tea	fur
spices	lions

☿ LEGACY

The moveable rudder for steering a ship was an important Chinese invention. It is used all over the world today.

Do ⊠ Discuss ⊠ Discover

1. Examine the model of the junk. With a partner, discuss the importance of the junk to the economic life of the ancient Chinese.

2. Look at the exports and imports on the chart. Select three of these products and explain, in your notes, what uses ancient cultures would have for each product.

Using Your Learning

Knowledge and Understanding

1. Find examples of ancient Chinese technology. Make a chart like the one below to include in your notebooks.

Economic Life	Technology (Types/Uses)
Farming	
Irrigation	
Fishing	
Mining	
Trade	
Arts/Crafts	

EXAMPLE

2. Write definitions and make sketches for your vocabulary words for this chapter. File your words in your Vocabulary File.

Inquiry/Research and Communication Skills

3. Find out more about camels. What other characteristics make them ideal animals for travel in harsh environments? Make a feature page about camels for your notes.

4. Find out about farming activities in your region of Canada. Make a farming calendar for your region like the Chinese calendar found on page 104 to show these activities.

Application

5. With a partner, discuss difficulties the traders travelling on the Silk Road might have encountered. In your notes, describe a journey on the Silk Road from the perspective of a trader.

6. In your notes, make a collage showing the kinds of work done by ancient Chinese people. Add labels to your collage.

7. Use a graphic organizer to compare technology in ancient China with technology in Canada today.

Section II Project

Chapters 8 and 9 focused on economic life in ancient China. In your project groups, refer back to the sub-headings in these chapters. Discuss what you have learned about the economic life of the ancient Chinese. Decide what kinds of pictures, illustrations, artifacts, models, skits, or oral explanations you will need to describe this part of the ancient Chinese culture in your documentary. Share the tasks among your group.

economic life · social life · political life · culture · the environment

Chapter 10
Social Structure

The social structure in ancient China was highly organized. People were born into different social classes. Roles were not very flexible, and change was difficult. Men could improve their social position through education and work. Family relationships were very important.

Focus on Learning

In this chapter you will learn about
- the different social classes in ancient China
- family life in ancient China
- language and education in ancient China
- writing a biography
- Chinese thinkers and inventors

Vocabulary

hierarchy	astrologer	innovation
status	characters	Daoism
rank	calligraphy	imperial
ancestor	Confucius	

Social Structure

People in ancient China lived within a **hierarchy**. A hierarchy is a system of levels based on importance. People in a hierarchy are considered less important than those above them and more important than those below them. In ancient China, this was true in social class, in the army, in the government, and in the family.

People were born into a certain social class. Change was not easy. There were two main ways to improve your **status**. (Status was where a person stood in the social structure.) One way was to show superior fighting ability in wartime. The other was to move up in the hierarchy as a public official in the government.

The government had many levels, or **ranks**. You could rise in status if you worked hard and were skilled at political life.

Social Class

Highest Class

Nobles, landowners, and scholars were respected for their power, wealth, land, and knowledge. Nobles usually came from families who had gathered land and wealth through family connections or success in war. If they supported the emperor, they kept their lands and titles.

Peasants were respected because they provided food for all of the people, but they were often poor. They were an essential part of the culture. They also paid taxes and worked on government programs such as road and canal building.

Artisans were respected because they made things that people needed, such as tools, weapons, and household items. They also made luxury items. Useful and beautiful things were valued in ancient Chinese culture.

Lowest Class

Merchants were considered to be in the lowest class because they did not produce anything essential. They made profits from buying and selling products that were the work of others. Although they had low status, merchants were often wealthy.

Family Life

Ancestors and family were extremely important in ancient China. Respect for your ancestors (your deceased family members) was one of the most important values of the people of ancient China. They believed that the spirits of the ancestors could protect them and help them be successful.

Usually at least three generations of a man's family lived together in the same home. Older family members were shown great respect. The oldest man was the head of the family.

Families had strict rules for behaviour. Younger people were required to respect and obey older people. Women had to respect and obey men.

The family was responsible for how its members conducted themselves. They had to punish those who did not behave appropriately.

Marriage

Marriages were arranged by families or by professional matchmakers. Sometimes marriages were arranged before the bride and groom were born. Different groups had different customs. Some brides were given dowries by their families. Other times, the groom's family paid a bride-price to the bride's family.

The wedding day was carefully chosen to ensure that the couple would have good fortune. Families often hired an **astrologer** to choose a favourable date. Astrologers studied the stars and made calculations and predictions.

The bride wore red, a symbol of happiness. She wore a veil all day. No one saw her face except her new husband.

In her husband's family, a new wife was the person with the lowest status. She had to be respectful and obedient. After she and her husband had a son, she became more important.

Men had one main wife, but they were allowed to have secondary wives if they could afford to support a large household.

Roles of Men and Women

Within the family, men had higher status than women and children. However, they were expected to respect and obey their own parents and elders. Men worked to provide most of the income to support their families.

A woman served and obeyed her husband and his family. She cooked, did household chores, and looked after the children. Many women also contributed to the family income through their work. For example, women raised silkworms and produced and embroidered fine silk fabric.

Children

Children were taught to be polite and to respect and obey their parents, grandparents, and all elders. They were expected to think of ways to help their elders without being asked.

Babies in ancient China were age one as soon as they were born! It was considered to be their first birthday.

Children helped with some household tasks, such as sweeping floors. Children of peasants, artisans, and other workers helped their parents work. For example, farm children chased birds out of the family crops.

Toys and Games

Children in ancient China played indoor and outdoor games. Some examples of their toys were rag dolls, puzzles, miniature clay or wooden replicas of objects, and musical instruments.

Kites made from brightly painted silk, paper, and bamboo were popular. Kites were made in shapes like birds, fish, dragonflies, or warriors.

Do ⊠ Discuss ⊠ Discover

1. With a partner, discuss how the expectations for children of ancient China compare with the expectations for children in your culture. Make a comparison chart for your notes to show your thinking.

Make a Kite

You will need

- ruler, pencil, scissors
- black marker
- paintbrush
- 12 bamboo skewers (25 cm)
- 11 m string
- large paper (70 cm x 50 cm)
- several colours of paint
- fibre tape
- large plastic garbage bag
- 15 cm piece of dowel

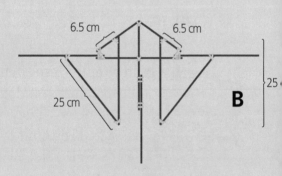

1. Measure and draw the kite outline onto paper and cut it out. Draw your design in pencil, outline it with black marker, and paint it bright colours.

2. To build the frame, first make a long rod by overlapping and taping three skewers together. Then, tape two skewers together to make a centre rod. Then, tape these two long rods in a cross, as shown in diagram A.

3. Cut two pieces to form a triangle between the top of the cross and the two sides of the crosspiece. Tape them in place firmly.

4. Tape two skewers at one end to form an angle. Attach the other ends to the top triangle and the crosspiece, as shown in diagram B. Do the same on the other side. (Do not tape the right angle crossings. The wings must be somewhat flexible.)

5. Attach two skewers at right angles to the ends of a 10 cm piece to form a U-shape. Attach the centre rod of the kite body to the base of the U, then tape the top ends of the U to the wing supports, as shown in diagram C.

6. Cut two 7 cm strips of plastic garbage bag 1.5 m long and attach them to the bottom of the frame to form kite tails.

7. Turn the painted kite over and fold a 1.5 cm edge along the tops of the wings and the top triangle. Wrap and tape the edges around the sides of the frame.

8. Make two holes through the kite—one where the centre rod attaches to the cross bar and one at the bottom skewer. Attach a 40 cm kite harness, then tie on the rest of the kite string and get ready to fly!

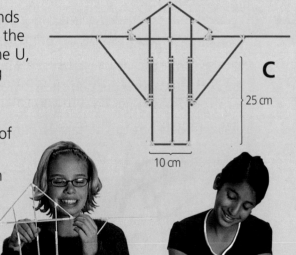

Language

The people of ancient China spoke many different dialects. Dialects are variations of the same language. Ancient Chinese words had one syllable, just like modern Chinese words.

In both ancient and modern Chinese, the same combination of sounds can have more than one meaning, depending on how the word is said. For example, the word *ma* spoken with a level tone means "mother." The same word spoken with a rising tone means "horse."

Writing

In the English language, the letters of the alphabet represent sounds. In traditional written Chinese, symbols called **characters** represented whole words or ideas. One historical dictionary listed about 40 000 different characters. To have the most basic level of literacy, a student had to learn to read and write at least 2000 characters.

Characters were drawn using a fine brush. The ink was made from the soot of burnt pinecones and glue. Characters were written vertically from top to bottom of the page and in columns from right to left.

This modern hanging presents a poem about the weather in elegant calligraphy.

Calligraphy is an artistic form of writing. The ancient Chinese drew their characters very precisely as a form of art.

	Sun	Moon	Tree	Bird
About 1500 BCE				
Before 213 BCE				
After 200 CE				

The earliest Chinese writing used pictures to represent words. Over the years, these pictures were simplified to symbols.

Do ⊠ Discuss ⊠ Discover

1. With a partner, discuss how the Chinese language is different from the English language. What do you think might be difficult about learning to use the Chinese language? Describe your thinking in your notebook.

2. Discuss the differences between using letters or characters to write your language. Which would you prefer? Explain your reasoning.

Education

The ancient Chinese believed that education was very important. Public and private schools for boys were established in parts of China during the Han dynasty. Families that could afford it sent their sons to school.

At school, boys learned astronomy and astrology, the teachings of the great teacher Kong Fuzi, literature, art, and music. Kong Fuzi is commonly known by the English version of his name, **Confucius**. Students who wanted positions in the government service memorized his writings.

The children of wealthy nobles did not attend schools. They studied at home with private tutors.

Most families could not afford to educate their sons. Boys were often needed to work on the land or learn the skills of their father's trade.

Girls did not go to school. They learned their mothers' skills in the home. Some girls also learned music, painting, and crafts from their mother or a woman tutor. Some girls learned to read and write, but they could not hold government jobs.

The daughter of a herbalist learned her mother's knowledge of herbs and healing.

This example of calligraphy says, "Study well. Get better every day." It is often seen in Chinese school classrooms today.

Do ⊠ Discuss ⊠ Discover

1. In your notes, make and label pictures showing the different ways that children in ancient China were educated.

2. In groups of two or three, discuss why you think that the ancient Chinese established public schools. Explain your reasons.

Writing a Biography

A biography is a true story about a person's life. When you write a biography, you need to give facts about your subject and the events in that person's life. The steps below will help you to write a biography.

1. Research your subject's life story thoroughly. Use a variety of reliable and current sources such as books, encyclopedias, magazines, videos, or the Internet.

2. Take notes as you find information and record the sources that you use.

3. Check your facts in different sources to make sure that they are accurate. If your sources disagree, explain the differences.

4. Find out about the places where your subject lived.

5. Learn about the culture and historical time period in which your subject lived.

6. Write a clear and interesting story that includes information about important facts and events in your subject's life. Include such facts as his or her birth, death, education, occupation, and accomplishments.

7. Write the facts honestly and fairly. Don't let your feelings or opinions cause you to portray your subject unfairly.

8. Edit the biography thoroughly and complete a final draft. You may want to include photos, charts, or illustrations to add interest to your story.

Ban Zhao

During the Han dynasty in China, it was unusual for women to have opportunities for education or to have a career. However, a woman named Ban Zhao came to be highly respected as a writer, historian, and tutor.

Ban Zhao's family served the Emperor as important government officials. Her great-grandfather had been invited to join the Emperor's court in the capital city, Chang'an, before Ban Zhao was born.

Ban Zhao's father was a scholar who was writing a long history of the Han dynasty in China. He owned a large library of books that had been given to him by an earlier emperor. He used them for his research.

One of Ban Zhao's brothers became an important military official. He travelled far into the frontiers where China bordered on other lands. Her other brother became a scholar like their father.

As a girl, Ban Zhao was interested in many things. She learned to read and write and developed a love for learning. She spent her days in the family library learning about the life and ideas of Confucius and reading poetry and other literature.

Sadly, when Ban Zhao was still very young, her father died. He had not been able to complete his history of the Han dynasty. Ban Zhao's brother promised to finish their father's huge project. She wanted to help him, but she was too young.

It was a young woman's duty to marry and have children. At the age of 14, Ban Zhao was married to a man whose family lived in a neighbouring region. She went to live with her husband's family, as was traditional.

They were married 20 years, then Ban Zhao's husband died. Her children were grown up, so Ban Zhao chose to return to live with her own family. This was very unusual. Normally a widow would continue to live with her husband's family.

Ban Zhao's son earned a job as a government official in eastern China. She travelled to live with him. Afterwards, she wrote a long poem about her experiences.

While she lived with her son in eastern China, Ban Zhao's brother died without finishing their father's history of the Han dynasty.

The Emperor sent a message to Ban Zhao asking her to complete the project! He had heard that Ban Zhao was well educated in history. Ban Zhao moved to the capital and worked in the Emperor's library. Eventually, she completed the huge project.

The Emperor was very pleased with her work and asked her to act as tutor to his young wife, the Empress. Ban Zhao also wrote books about the many things she had learned. During her life, she wrote 16 books.

Surprisingly, Ban Zhao held traditional views on the place of women in the social structure. She followed the teachings of Confucius. Confucius believed that women's most important roles were as daughters, wives, and mothers. However, Ban Zhao also believed that education for girls was important. Her life would have been very different if she had not had that opportunity.

Thinkers and Inventors

The writings and ideas of ancient Chinese thinkers influenced the way Chinese culture developed and changed. There were many great mathematicians, scientists, and inventors in ancient China. Some of their **innovations** (new ideas) contributed to many other cultures.

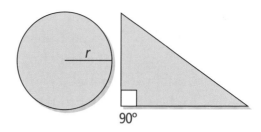

Zhang Heng also figured out an accurate way to determine the circumference and area of circles. Ancient Chinese mathematicians used right angle triangles to estimate distances across rivers.

Ancient Chinese alchemists, who were the earliest chemists, learned to make bronze and brass. Alchemists also discovered lodestone, a naturally magnetic stone. This led to the invention of the compass.

Ancient Chinese astronomers studied the stars, sun, and moon. They figured out that a year has 365.52 days and learned to predict the seasons. The astronomer and mathematician Zhang Heng developed the first seismograph for detecting earthquakes in 130 CE. It is shown above.

The philosopher Confucius believed in an orderly world based on hierarchy. His ideas about structure, responsibility, obedience, and respect in family life and society influenced Chinese culture for thousands of years.

Laozi was a philosopher who believed that all people should live in harmony with nature. His ideas formed the basis of a Chinese religion called **Daoism**. The Daoist *yin–yang* symbol shows the balance between dark and light forces in the natural world.

Do ▨ Discuss ▨ Discover

1. Choose an ancient Chinese thinker or inventor. Use the directions on page 123 to write a biography of the person you selected.

Paper

The invention of paper was announced in 105 CE by Cai Lun, a palace servant who was the leader of an **imperial** workshop. (Imperial means belonging to the emperor or to the empire.)

Paper was one of the most important Chinese innovations. It was first made from shredded silk rags. Later it came to be made of plant products like hemp, bark, or bamboo.

Paper has been used for writing since it was invented. The ancient Chinese found it to be light and portable. It needed less storage space than clay tablets or bamboo strips, which had been used in the past for writing on.

Paper was also quite inexpensive to make in large quantities, compared to parchment or silk scrolls. These had also been used in the past.

Paper was in great demand in the Han government service. It was needed for communication. They used it to keep records and send reports and messages. In later centuries in China, paper was also used for printing books and for making paper money.

Papermaking

1. The raw material was soaked in water to soften it, then boiled and pounded to make pulp.

2. A fine screen was dipped into the pulp to gather a thin film, lifted out carefully, and gently shaken.

3. The screen was pressed between absorbent surfaces to get the water out of the pulp fibres, then hung to dry.

4. When it was dry, the paper was carefully peeled off the screen. Then it was brushed to smooth the surface.

♀ LEGACY

Canada is one of the largest manufacturers of pulp and paper in the world today. Canada produces about half of the world's newsprint. About four-fifths of the paper produced here is exported.

The production of paper can be an environmental concern. Many programs today focus on making the pulp and paper industries safer for the environment. Paper recycling is one of the ways this environmental concern is being addressed.

Do ⊠ Discuss ⊠ Discover

1. With a small group, discuss why paper might be called one of the world's great inventions. In your notes, make a list of reasons that support this idea.

2. With a small group, do a scavenger hunt in your classroom to find as many examples as you can of ways that paper is used.

Using Your Learning

Knowledge and Understanding

1. Review page 117. In a small group, make a poster illustrating people from the different social classes in ancient China doing their jobs.

2. On a comparison chart, compare family life in ancient China with family life in your culture. Put your chart in your notes.

3. Write definitions and make sketches for the vocabulary words in this chapter in your Vocabulary File.

Inquiry/Research and Communication Skills

4. Use the Internet websites www.chinapage.org/china.html and www.mandarintools.com to find out more about the Chinese language. Find a Chinese translation for your name. Write it in your notes and explain its meaning.

5. Use the library or the Internet website www.crystalinks.com/chinainventions.html to review some Chinese inventions. Illustrate one of the inventions in your notebook and explain why you think that it is important.

Application

6. In small groups, take on the various roles of people living in ancient China. Develop interview questions concerning the lives of these people. Take turns interviewing each of the people in your group in their roles.

7. Imagine that you are living on an ancient Chinese farm. Make a daily schedule listing the jobs that need to be done. Include your schedule in your notebook.

8. Think about why family is important in a culture. In your notes, write your ideas about how the family helps the culture to grow and survive.

economic life
social life
political life
culture
the environment

Chapter 11
Religion, Arts, Sports

The ancient Chinese believed that everything in their culture needed to be in harmony with the natural world. These beliefs were reflected in all aspects of their lives. They sought to achieve harmony and balance in their religion, their arts, and even their physical activities.

Focus on Learning

In this chapter you will learn about
- the spiritual beliefs of the ancient Chinese
- the visual, literary, and performing arts of the ancient Chinese people
- Chinese architecture
- sports in ancient China

Vocabulary

ancestor-worship	scroll
Buddhism	*feng shui*
incense	martial arts

Religion

The oldest ancient Chinese religion was **ancestor-worship**. People believed that the spirits of their ancestors lived on after death and protected the family. They prayed to them and asked them for advice. Chinese homes had a special shrine for making offerings and communicating with the ancestors.

Buddhism was a religion that began in India around 500 BCE. The teachings of the Buddha were introduced to China during the Han dynasty.

Incense

The ancient Chinese made **incense** from the dust of sweet-smelling woods mixed with clay. They burned incense in ceremonies honouring their ancestors. The sticks burned slowly and filled the air with their perfume.

The Three Ways

The teachings of Confucius, the Buddha, and Laozi (Daoism) had many followers in ancient China. These were known as the "Three Ways." Confucianism was not a religion. However, these teachings influenced many parts of Chinese life.

Confucius (550–479 BCE)
Proper behaviour is necessary to have an orderly society. You must respect and honour your ancestors. People in authority have many responsibilities. Obey them so order is maintained. Everyone should know his or her place, work hard, and keep the peace.

Buddha (around 550 BCE)
People suffer in life because of wanting. They need to follow a way of life that frees them from wanting. Then they will have peace. Otherwise, when people die, they are born again and again until they finally learn these lessons.

Laozi (around 500 BCE)
Everything in nature must be in balance, including people. We must live simple lives close to nature. The natural world is divided into light and dark forces that are in balance with each other. We must try to maintain this harmony in our lives.

Burial Customs

The ancient Chinese believed that the spirits of the dead went to another world similar to their own world. Relatives needed to supply the spirits with possessions for the afterlife. They placed objects and clay models of things the spirits would need in the coffins or tomb.

Wealthy people in ancient China buried their dead in family tombs with stone lions to guard against evil spirits. They wrapped the bodies in silk. Some nobles were even buried in suits made from tiny pieces of jade. Poorer people placed their dead in clay coffins and buried them in shallow graves.

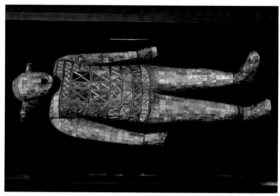

Jade was believed to last forever. This jade suit was meant to protect the body from decaying after death.

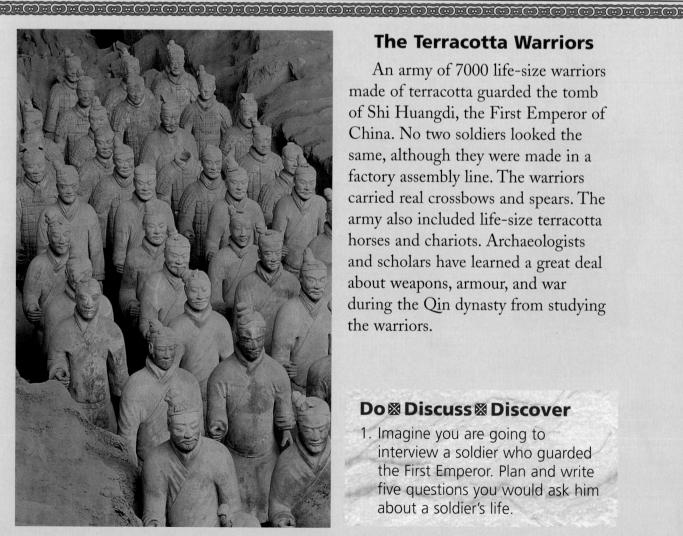

The Terracotta Warriors

An army of 7000 life-size warriors made of terracotta guarded the tomb of Shi Huangdi, the First Emperor of China. No two soldiers looked the same, although they were made in a factory assembly line. The warriors carried real crossbows and spears. The army also included life-size terracotta horses and chariots. Archaeologists and scholars have learned a great deal about weapons, armour, and war during the Qin dynasty from studying the warriors.

Do ⊠ Discuss ⊠ Discover

1. Imagine you are going to interview a soldier who guarded the First Emperor. Plan and write five questions you would ask him about a soldier's life.

The Arts

The Chinese have produced magnificent works of art for thousands of years. In ancient times, the educated upper class of people had wealth to buy beautiful things. They also had leisure time to appreciate them.

Han metalworkers produced beautiful containers and utensils from bronze. Most were used in ceremonies.

Artists produced works of calligraphy, painting, sculpture, and embroidery. Authors wrote poetry, stories, and philosophy. Dancers, musicians, and entertainers performed for both the wealthy and the poor.

Painters also created splendid murals for the walls of tombs or important buildings. Murals often showed scenes from history or legends.

Sculpture was also an important art. Sculptors worked in stone, fired clay, bronze, and other materials. They created guardian figures to protect tombs, religious statues such as Buddha figures, and artworks like the flying horse on the left for homes and palaces.

Artisans made jewellery, ornaments, ceremonial objects, and furniture from rich materials. Potters covered their clay pieces with deep, brilliant glazes.

Scenes from nature, mythical animals and symbols, and people were common subjects of art.

A censer like this one was filled with sand to hold up sticks of burning incense.

Visual Arts

Ancient Chinese artists painted delicate images on silk hangings or long rolled paper **scrolls**. The brush strokes were controlled and graceful, like Chinese calligraphy. Most paintings were about nature or showed people in a landscape. Silk and paper are fragile. Very few Qin and Han dynasty works on these materials have survived.

Do ✶ Discuss ✶ Discover

1. Look at the examples of Chinese art on this page. Discuss with a partner what you can learn about life in ancient China from these examples.

Literary Arts

Written works were copied by hand and writings were very valuable. The earliest books were written on strips of bamboo that were bundled together. Scrolls of silk and paper were used later, before bound paper books came into use.

During the Qin dynasty, Emperor Shi Huangdi burned many written works. The ideas in them were different from his way of thinking. He kept books about "practical subjects," but no poetry or philosophy.

During the Han dynasty that followed, writers and scribes worked hard to restore the literature that had been destroyed. The works of Confucius were particularly important.

The first national library was built during the Han dynasty. It included the written works of many important Chinese thinkers, scientists, and scholars.

Poetry

Poets in ancient China were often inspired by the beauty of nature. They used examples from nature to express their feelings about human life.

Poems were usually written in delicate calligraphy. Many were illustrated with painting. Poets recited or sang their poems to friends.

Mythology

Chinese mythology included stories explaining the beginning of the world and the reasons for natural phenomena like rainbows.

One Chinese myth tells of the goddess Nu Wa modelling human figures from mud. She set the tiny figures on the Earth and they became the rich nobles. When she became tired of this activity, she scattered the leftover bits of mud. These became the poor people of China.

This portrait of the poet Tao Yuan Ming (365–427 CE) was painted with a brush and ink on a paper scroll.

Performing Arts

People of ancient China enjoyed many kinds of performances. Popular forms of entertainment included dancing, musical presentations, plays, magic shows, and displays of acrobatics and martial arts.

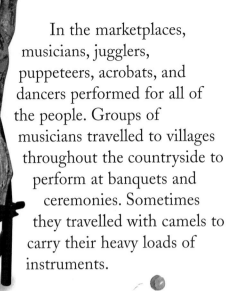

Wealthy people often employed musicians in their homes. Musicians played bells, gongs, drums, metal or stone chimes, bamboo flutes, and silk-stringed zithers. Dancers wearing elegant gowns and jugglers or acrobats performed to music at banquets or ceremonies.

During the Han dynasty, a special music department was set up to collect songs and musical compositions.

In the marketplaces, musicians, jugglers, puppeteers, acrobats, and dancers performed for all of the people. Groups of musicians travelled to villages throughout the countryside to perform at banquets and ceremonies. Sometimes they travelled with camels to carry their heavy loads of instruments.

Puppetry

Puppetry originated in China. Entertainers used puppets to tell stories in the marketplaces, at the imperial court, or at special events. One Chinese emperor placed large puppets around the palace to fool an attacking army into thinking that he was present in the palace.

133

Mulan

About 1500 years ago, tribes of horse-riding Asians called Huns swept into China from the north. The Emperor called his armies together to defend the country. One male from each family would have to serve in the army to fight against the Huns. In villages and towns all over China, families received notice of conscription from the Emperor.

Mulan's brother was very young and her father was elderly and in poor health. She was afraid that her father would die if he had to serve in the army.

One morning as Mulan was working in the garden, she saw an imperial messenger arrive. As she had feared—her father had been ordered to present himself for military service!

That night Mulan could not sleep. How could she prevent her father from having to go into battle? What could she do? She was not a man! Suddenly Mulan was struck with an idea. Maybe she could disguise herself as a young man and go in her father's place.

She slipped quietly from her bed, tied her hair back, and dressed in her father's armour. She took her father's sword and his notice from the Emperor. With tears in her eyes, Mulan said a silent good-bye to her family and left to take her father's place in the imperial army.

Mulan reached the army camp and presented herself to the captain in charge. The captain assigned her to a training group. No one suspected that she was really a girl, and she learned to fight fiercely and skillfully.

Over the years, Mulan fought in many battles to defend the country. Her superior skills as a soldier were greatly admired by her commanders. She fought like the warriors in the old legends.

Finally, after many successful battles, the soldiers in Mulan's company were allowed to return to their homes. The Emperor summoned Mulan to court.

He had learned about this brave soldier's accomplishments. He decided to reward her, so he offered her an important government position.

Mulan knew that she could not continue to pose as a man in order to take the post. She wished to return to her family. She refused the Emperor's position.

The Emperor was disappointed. However, he said to Mulan, "You have been very brave and deserve a reward. I will give you one of my finest horses to thank you for your service."

Mulan accepted the valuable horse as her reward and returned to her family.

Years later, some soldiers who had been in battle with Mulan came to visit the family. They were the first to discover that the warrior they had fought with was really a woman!

Architecture

Chinese architecture is distinctive. The style of walled homes common during the Han dynasty developed in a time when landowners had to be prepared for attack at any time. Family living quarters, gardens, kitchens, and servants' quarters were separate.

A strong wall, usually with a watchtower, surrounded the whole set of buildings. Strangers came in only as far as the gatehouse or a waiting area. (The illustration on page 96 shows an example.)

The environment affected architecture. Buildings were raised above the ground for protection from the damp earth. Heavy overhanging roofs protected buildings from heavy rain and hot sun. Roofs were supported by a network of sturdy wooden beams. This allowed movement during an earthquake so the roof would not collapse.

The roofs of buildings were made of decorative tiles. Glazed pottery guardian creatures and symbols helped to protect the building from evil spirits.

Very important buildings such as the imperial palaces were surrounded by magnificent gardens. They were hidden from public view by brightly painted walls and majestic gateways.

The three sections of this Han dynasty model of a tower stack on each other.

The Emperor's palace in the capital city Chang'an was enclosed in a strong wall.

Feng Shui

Feng shui is a set of rules and practices for ensuring that all things in the environment are in perfect harmony. The ancient Chinese believed it was important to choose carefully where and how a building would be situated. The perfect placement of a building would bring protection and good fortune to the people living in it. A bad choice of design, such as where a door or stairway was placed, could allow misfortune into the house or let goodness flow away.

Do ⊠ Discuss ⊠ Discover

1. Look at illustrations and pictures of Chinese and Greek architecture in this textbook. Use a comparison chart to note the similarities and differences.

2. Describe examples of Chinese architecture in your community or in photographs you have seen.

Sports and Recreation

The people of ancient China enjoyed sports. Both men and women participated in physical activities. They played such games as catch, tug of war, and a kind of football using a ball made from silk. Women also liked to compete to see who could reach the greatest height on swings.

Martial Arts

Martial arts were popular in ancient China for exercise and self-defence. Martial arts are skills learned for fighting. *Taiji* and *gongfu* are modern examples of Chinese martial arts.

Taiji involves a series of slow graceful movements that are used for defense. The movements are based on the Daoist *yin–yang* philosophy of balance between opposing forces.

Gongfu, another martial art, is a form of boxing. It involves kicks, turns, strikes with the hand, leaps, and somersaults.

Dragon Boat Festival

The Dragon Boat Festival dates back to ancient times. Legend says that a local king banished a court official named Qu Yuan, who was much loved by the people. Qu Yuan wandered the countryside reciting his poetry. Finally he became so depressed that he threw himself into a river. Fishers rushed to try to save him but failed. Since that time, on the fifth day of the fifth month, dragon boat races have been held in memory of Qu Yuan.

Teams of rowers compete in Dragon Boat Races in Canadian cities. These races are often held to support charitable causes.

Dragon Boat Races are held in Vancouver's harbour.

The Toronto Dragon Boat Race in June 2000 was an exciting event.

Using Your Learning

Knowledge and Understanding

1. Make a web in your notes like the one shown below. Complete the web with details from this chapter.

2. Add the words from this chapter to your Vocabulary File. Remember to include definitions and sketches.

Inquiry/Research and Communication Skills

3. Like Chinese, English can be written using calligraphy. In the library or at the websites www.chinapage.com/ calligraphy.html or www.mandarintools.com, learn more about the art of calligraphy. Try writing examples of English letters or words in calligraphy.

4. Chinese poetry was often inspired by feelings about nature. Think about things in nature that are important to you. Write and illustrate a poem that expresses your feelings about one of these things.

Application

5. Plan a Chinese festival of the Arts. Consider what you will need to include in order to show the ancient Chinese culture. Use the sub-titles on pages 131 to 135 as a guide. Make a poster advertising the festival.

6. In a small group, discuss how the invention of paper has influenced the world. With your group, create a collage or a display to demonstrate the many uses of paper.

Section II Project

Chapters 10 and 11 focused on the social life of ancient China. With your group, review these chapters and your notes. Decide what you will need to prepare for your documentary to describe key information about social life. As a group, prepare the artifacts, illustrations, stories, skits, and other means of presentation that you will use.

Chapter 12
Political Life

In 221 BCE, the kingdoms of ancient China were **unified** into a single empire. The government was a hereditary monarchy led by an emperor. A huge number of public officials were paid to assist the emperor in running the country. The people had no say in choosing their leaders or style of government. People paid taxes, served in the army, and provided labour on public works as part of their duty to the state.

Focus on Learning

In this chapter you will learn about
• the Chinese Empire
• the capital city
• government in ancient China
• the legal system
• writing a news article
• how the ancient Chinese defended themselves

Vocabulary

unified	influence
ward	magistrate
merit	garrison

The Chinese Empire

Before 200 BCE, China was a collection of small states at war with each other. During the Qin dynasty (221 BCE–206 BCE), these states were unified to form one very large country under the first emperor, Qin Shi Huangdi. The Qin dynasty only lasted for a few years and was followed by the Han dynasty (202 BCE–220 CE). Many more dynasties followed. China was an empire for over 2100 years.

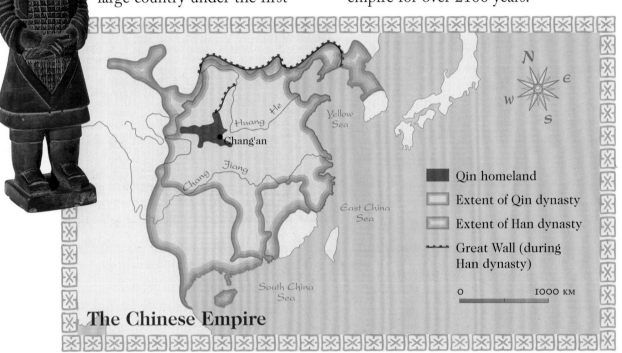

Qin homeland

Extent of Qin dynasty

Extent of Han dynasty

Great Wall (during Han dynasty)

0   1000 KM

The Chinese Empire

The First Emperor

China's name comes from the Qin (pronounced Chin) dynasty. A war leader of the Qin kingdom named Ying Zheng conquered other kingdoms until he controlled all of China. He called himself Shi Huangdi, "the First Emperor."

Shi Huangdi made strict laws and taxed everyone. He was feared rather than loved, but he accomplished many things for China. He built roads and canals to improve communication. He created a common form of writing, money, and measurement to be used throughout China.

The other noble families were forced to be responsible for law and order in their regions. They had to enforce the Emperor's commands.

Qin Shi Huangdi planned a huge burial monument for himself. The terracotta warriors shown on page 130 were part of his memorial. It took 40 years to complete.

The Capital City

China had about 57 million people during the Han dynasty. There were a number of cities, but most of the people lived in rural villages and towns.

The city of Chang'an (now called Xian) became the imperial capital during the Han dynasty. It was located on a river that flowed into the Huang He. Chang'an was a centre of government, education, and trade.

Like most Chinese cities, Chang'an was designed in the shape of a square and built on a grid plan. The Emperor and his court lived in the centre and south part of the city. The city was surrounded by a strong wall made of earth and stone for protection.

In the 700s CE, Chang'an was the biggest city in the world.

Chang'an continued to be the capital city several centuries after the Han dynasty. The diagram above shows how the city was divided into sections called **wards** in later centuries. Wealthy people and nobles lived in luxury in certain wards. Others held government buildings. Poorer people, like the imperial craftspeople, lived in crowded tangles of small houses. Merchants lived outside the walls of the city.

Lower Class Ward | Government Buildings | Palace
Middle Class Ward | Markets
Upper Class Ward | Offices

The Government

The government of ancient China was a hereditary monarchy. The emperor ruled by right of birth. A huge number of public officials were paid to manage the day-to-day running of the empire.

The Emperor

The emperor was at the top of the hierarchy, or levels of power. The people believed that he was a "Son of Heaven" who had special powers from Heaven.

The emperor was expected to rule fairly and care for his people. However, his people rarely saw him. Only senior public officials, the generals of the army, and the imperial family had personal contact with him.

The emperor and his family lived in the capital city of Chang'an. Their grand palace was surrounded by gardens full of rare plants and animals. Thousands of palace servants and officials worked to entertain and inform him.

Imperial Government Officials

Most government business was carried out by public officials. The government service was highly structured. There were many different ranks with different powers and responsibilities. Some officials worked for the central government in Chang'an and others worked in country towns and villages.

Taxation to pay for public works was introduced in China around 200 BCE.

During the Han dynasty, people got jobs in the civil service partly through **merit** and partly through **influence**. Merit means deserving something because of one's abilities. Influence means having a more powerful person recommend you. In later centuries, men had to pass several levels of strict government examinations. Many more competed for the jobs than were hired. It was important to have a senior member of government use his influence and recommend you for a position.

A Change of Fortune

Wu Mantian lived with his family in an apartment above a tiny shop. In the shop, his grandfather and father made fine shoes, boots, and sandals for people of the town.

Wu Mantian's grandmother and mother were known for their embroidery on silk. Their beautiful work was greatly sought after by well-to-do people to make into clothing.

Wu Mantian was learning his father and grandfather's trade. He prepared the leather, hemp, or silk they used to craft the footwear that the family sold.

The family hoped to send Wu Mantian to school. Few boys could be spared from working in family businesses, even for a short time. However, Wu Mantian's father was able to read. All his life he had studied the works of Confucius after his work in the shop was done. He wanted his son to share his love of knowledge and ideas, as well as be a good shoemaker.

Wu Mantian often walked past the great homes of the wealthy public officials. He marveled at the decorated roofs and brightly painted walls around these homes. He peeked through the gates for glimpses of wonderful gardens full of flowers and shrubs.

Sai Jixian, an important government official, lived in one of these homes. Sai Jixian frequently visited the Wu family shop. He bought shoes and boots there for his family. Wu Mantian's grandmother and mother created colourful symbols of peacocks, butterflies, and flowers on silk for his family's clothing.

When Sai Jixian's visited the Wu family shop, he often spent time discussing ideas with Wu Mantian's father, Wu Wolong. Although Sai Jixian belonged to a much higher social class, he came to greatly admire Wu Wolong for his wisdom and knowledge. He knew Wu Wolong devoted much of his spare time to reading and thinking about the ideas of Confucius.

On one of Sai Jixian's visits to the imperial court in Chang'an, he spoke about Wu Wolong to several of the Emperor's highest officials. "In a small town in my region, there lives a shoemaker who is a brilliant scholar of the teachings of Confucius. I believe that the Emperor would benefit greatly from this man's service."

In time, the brilliance of Wu Wolong was brought to the Emperor's attention. Then, one day Sai Jixian arrived at the Wu family shop. Wu Mantian's father and grandfather bowed low to Sai Jixian. Then, Sai Jixian presented Wu Mantian's father with a scroll bearing the Emperor's seal!

The scroll summoned Wu Wolong to join the Emperor's civil service. Wu Mantian's father proudly accepted the challenge of his new occupation. The friendship between Wu Wolong and Sai Jixian had changed the fortunes of the Wu family forever.

Instead of a life making shoes and boots, like his grandfather and father, Wu Mantian could now look forward to a Confucian education and the opportunity for a position in the Emperor's civil service.

The Legal System

In ancient China, there were strict rules that controlled the social structure. Obedience within a family was expected. The family was held responsible for the behaviour of its members. If a person committed a crime, the authorities could punish the family.

Magistrates were the public officials who enforced the laws and judged court cases. The magistrates had many responsibilities. They collected taxes, supervised building projects, and inspected schools. They also registered births, deaths, marriages, and property.

Court officials called censors investigated cases of injustice or poor government. They collected evidence to prove a person guilty of a crime. The magistrate sentenced the person to an appropriate type of punishment based on the evidence.

Punishments ranged from being whipped or locked up to being put to death. Execution could be quick, such as being beheaded, or slow and painful.

The crane was a symbol of justice. Magistrates often had images of cranes in their courtrooms.

Do ⊠ Discuss ⊠ Discover

1. With a partner, discuss what is meant by "crimes of injustice or poor government." Recall what you have learned about the ancient Chinese culture. What are two possible examples of these crimes? Explain your reasons.

2. Use a Venn diagram to compare the legal systems of ancient China and ancient Greece.

Writing a News Article

A news article is a brief piece of writing that describes a factual event. An article must provide the reader with a clear understanding of what happened and who was involved in the event.

In order to help your readers understand the importance of an event, you should describe

- the event and important circumstances surrounding it
- the factors that caused it
- the consequences or outcomes

A news article needs to answer certain questions for the reader. The following questions are a guide for providing the necessary information in a news article.

WHO?   Name the people involved in the event.
WHAT?   Describe the particulars of the event and how it happened.
WHERE?   Identify the location of the event.
WHEN?   Tell when the event took place.
WHY?   Explain the reasons for the event.

Look at articles in a newspaper to find examples of how writers have answered the *who*, *what*, *where*, *when*, and *why* questions.

Do ☒ Discuss ☒ Discover

1. Examine the picture of the court case on page 143. With a partner, speculate on what the crime was, what evidence existed, what the judge was thinking, and the verdict. Write a news article about this case.

Defense and War

In China's early history, separate states were often at war with one another. Their leaders raised large armies and fought each other for land, wealth, and control.

States also defended themselves against invading armies from other powers to the north and west. After the Chinese states were unified, China still needed protection from invasion. Bands of horse-riding warriors from other parts of Asia were a constant danger.

During the Han dynasty, all able-bodied men were conscripted to serve in the army without pay for two years. They were supplied with food, weapons, and armour. They were sent to live in a **garrison**, or army post, far from home until their military service was finished. After that they could be called to join the army again whenever they were needed.

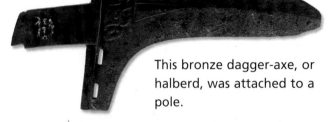

The Chinese army sometimes used kites to frighten their enemies.

Chinese soldiers were well equipped for battle. They had bows and arrows, crossbows, swords, halberds (long blades on poles), and horses.

This bronze dagger-axe, or halberd, was attached to a pole.

The Great Wall

The first sections of the defensive stone wall known later as the Great Wall of China were built about 435 BCE. The wall and its watchtowers were used to protect China against invasion. The sections were extended and connected during the reign of the First Emperor, about 214 BCE. The wall continued to be maintained and sections rebuilt until about 1600 CE.

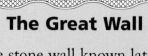

The Great Wall stretched for approximately 5000 km along China's northern border. A road ran along the top of the wall. In most places, it was wide enough for five horses to be ridden side by side.

Soldiers were stationed at the watchtowers. Watchtowers were the distance of two arrow shots apart. Soldiers communicated with each other by signalling with flags during the day and torches at night. It was lonely and uncomfortable duty.

The Great Wall is the longest structure in the world. It is a major tourist site visited by millions today.

Do ⊠ Discuss ⊠ Discover

1. In a small group, discuss what it would be like to visit the Great Wall. What would you see and do there? Make an itinerary for your trip and put it in your notes.

Using Your Learning

Knowledge and Understanding

1. Carefully examine the illustration for political life on page 138. Write a story about the picture. Include information about political life that is shown in the illustration.

2. With a partner, discuss how political life contributed to the great empire that was built by the ancient Chinese. Write point form notes outlining your ideas.

3. Add the vocabulary words from this chapter to your Vocabulary File. Choose one of the following activities to complete your vocabulary study for ancient China:
   • Create a picture dictionary.
   • Make up word games (e.g., riddles, matching words, and definitions).
   • Design crossword puzzles or word searches.

Inquiry/Research and Communication Skills

4. The Great Wall was built to protect the Chinese people from invaders from Mongolia. Use an encyclopedia to find out more about these invaders. Write a brief description for your notes.

5. China was an empire during the Qin and Han dynasties. Make a chart that compares a government ruled by an emperor with the form of government in Canada today.

Application

6. With a partner, brainstorm what life would have been like for a poor family living in one of China's cities. Imagine that you are a member of such a family. Write a description of your life.

7. Compare the city of Chang'an with a city that you know in Canada. Use a Venn diagram to indicate similarities and differences.

Section II Project

In Chapter 12, you focused on the political life of the ancient Chinese. With your group, review this chapter and make decisions about how you will provide information about political life. Share the tasks of preparing to show this part of the culture. Use such presentation techniques as maps, illustrations, skits or role-plays, artifacts, illustrations, or photos.

Timeline Activity

With your project group, refer to the timeline for China inside the front cover of the book. Locate the time period for the Qin and Han dynasties. Make and illustrate a timeline for this period of Chinese history.

Legacies from the Past

Legacies from past civilizations have contributed to our culture in many ways. These ancient civilizations have influenced

- how we think and live
- ideas about science, technology, and mathematics
- the arts of today
- the languages we speak
- many of today's religious beliefs

Do ⊠ Discuss ⊠ Discover

1. Examine the pictures on this page. Identify contributions from early civilizations that these pictures represent.

Section II Project

Complete and share your Section II Project. Follow the sequence below.

- Work with your project group to complete your Historical Documentary about ancient China, and prepare to present it.

- Use the Model for Learning about a Civilization on pages 4 and 5 as a guide in planning your presentation. Show how the environment and economic, social, and political life in ancient China were related.

- Review the presentation materials that you developed or gathered while you were studying ancient China. Plan how you will organize and present the various kinds of information in an interesting way.

- Use the History Wall of ancient Greece you created in Section I to make comparisons between the ancient civilizations of Greece and China. Make this part of your presentation.

- Decide how you will share the various parts of your presentation among the members of your group. Refer to Making an Oral Presentation on page 108 and Role-play on page 49. They can help you prepare for your part of the presentation.

- Plan how you will share your Historical Documentary with others. Some possibilities are to make presentations to your class, to other classes, or to adults in your community. If you have access to a video camera, you might tape your documentary to share with your family or other interested people.

Pronunciation Guide

The accented syllable is underlined. All vowels are short except the following:

ay = long a (make)
y = long i (like)
oo = long u (mule)
ee = long e (equal)
oh = long o (rope)

Greece

Acropolis (a <u>kro</u> poh lis)
Aesculapius (ehs coo <u>lay</u> pi us)
agoraphobia (a gro <u>foh</u> bi a)
Aphrodite (af ro <u>dy</u> tee)
Apollo (a <u>pol</u> loh)
Archimedes (ar ki <u>mee</u> dees)
Ares (<u>ay</u> res)
Aristotle (a ri <u>sto</u> tle)
Artemis (<u>ar</u> te mis)
Athene (a <u>thee</u> nee)
Charon (<u>ka</u> ron)
chiton (<u>ky</u> ton)
Demeter (de <u>mee</u> ter)
Eros (<u>er</u> ohs)
Hades (<u>hay</u> dees)
Hephaestus (he <u>fys</u> tus)
Hera (<u>he</u> ra)
Hermes (<u>her</u> mees)
Hestia (hes <u>ti</u> a)
himation (hi <u>may</u> shon)
Hippocrates (hi <u>po</u> kre tees)
Parthenon (<u>par</u> thi non)
Pericles (<u>peh</u> ri klees)
Plato (<u>play</u> toh)
Poseidon (<u>poh</u> sy don)
Socrates (<u>so</u> kre tees)
Zeus (<u>zooss</u>)

China

Ban Zhao (ban zhaoh)
Beijing (bay jing)
Cai Lun (chai lun)
Chang Jiang (chang jiang)
Chang'an (chang an)
Daoism (dau ism)
feng shui (feng sh wee)
Heilong Jiang (hay long jiang)
Huang He (hwung heh)
Kong Fuzi (kong foo tsee)
Laozi (laoh tsee)
Nu Wa (noo wa)
Qin (chin)
Qu Yuan (chu yooan)
Sai Jixian (sy jissyan)
Shi Huangdi (shee hwung dee)
taiji (ty jee)
Wu Mantian (woo man tyan)
Wu Wolong (woo woh loong)
Xian (see an)
Zhang Heng (zhang heng)

Glossary

A

acupuncture—a medical treatment using sharp, thin needles to stimulate forces to heal the body or block pain

administration—management; the work that government officials do to provide government services

agora—(Greek) central public marketplace where most business and many other activities took place

alchemist—a scientist in ancient times who studied chemistry

ancestor—a deceased family member

ancestor-worship—belief that the spirits of ancestors protect and help people

apprentice—a young person working with a skilled adult to learn and become qualified at a trade or craft

aquaculture—raising freshwater or saltwater fish in tanks or ponds as a food source

aqueduct—an artificial channel carrying water

artifacts—objects or physical evidence of how people of the past lived

artisan—a skilled person who produces arts and finely made objects

astrologer—a person who studies the stars and makes calculations and predictions

astronomer—a scientist who studies the stars, planets, moon, and sun

B

brazier—a metal pan with a grill, often placed on a metal stand, used for heat or cooking

bronze—a metal made from a mixture of metals, mainly copper and tin

Buddhism—a religion that originated in India, based on the teachings of the Buddha

C

calligraphy—an artistic form of writing

capital—decorated top of a column that holds up a roof

characters—symbols representing words or ideas used to write Chinese and some other Asian languages

chiton—a garment worn in ancient Greece made of a large rectangular piece of cloth fastened over the shoulders

citizen—in ancient Greece, free men and women whose parents had been born in the city-state

city-state—a city in ancient Greece, with its surrounding farmland, which formed an independent state with its own government

civilization—a group of people with an organized and technologically advanced culture

climate—the average weather pattern of a place over a long period; includes average temperatures, precipitation, wind patterns, humidity, and seasons

colony—land governed by another country that established settlements there

column—a pillar that supports a roof

Confucius—a Chinese philosopher whose ideas and writings greatly influenced beliefs about family life and society

conscription—being called up to do government service, such as work on public building projects or serve in the army

consequences—events that occur because of a previous action

contour line—a line connecting points on a map that have the same elevation

craftsperson—a skilled person who makes useful items

culture—all of the ways the people of a group meet their needs; a people's way of life

D

Daoism—a Chinese religion based on the writings of the philosopher Laozi, who believed that all people should live in harmony with nature

democracy—the citizens of a country vote to elect representatives who make decisions for the country

dictatorship—a government in which one powerful person takes control and makes decisions for all of the people

dowry—money or form of wealth given by a bride's family either to the bride or to the man she marries

dynasty—a historical period named after the ruling family of the time

E

economic life—the ways people make a living, including their food, shelter, clothing, health, occupations, technology, and trade

elevation—height above sea level; altitude

emperor—leader of an empire, usually by right of birth but sometimes by conquest

empire—a huge country, often made up of several formerly independent states

environment—the surrounding air, land, and water of a place, including landforms, bodies of water, climate, vegetation, animal life, and natural resources

export—to sell or trade a product to a distant place

F

fabric—woven cloth

feng shui—(ancient China) a set of rules and practices to ensure all things are in harmony

frieze—a band of sculpture or painting along a wall or around a room

G

garrison—an army post where soldiers lived, usually far from home

gorge—a steep-sided river valley

gymnasium—in ancient Greece, a sports complex where men went to exercise and use the bathing facilities

H

harmony—orderly beauty created through balanced relationships

hemp—a plant grown for the fibres in its stem, used to make rope or rough fabric

herbalist—a person who gathers and preserves herbs, and treats health conditions with herbs and other natural products

hereditary monarchy—a country where a king or queen governs by right of birth

hierarchy—groups arranged in levels according to importance

himation—a cloak made of wool worn by ancient Greeks

hoplite—an armoured soldier in ancient Greece who fought on foot

I

imperial—having to do with an empire or belonging to an emperor

import—to purchase and bring in a product from elsewhere

incense—sticks made from the dust of sweet-smelling wood mixed with clay, burned as part of a ceremony

independent—having a separate government or authority; not controlled by another

influence—to affect or change; to act on someone's behalf so that he or she will benefit

innovation—an invention, discovery, or new idea

irrigation—building canals or using technology to provide water for crops

J

jade—a hard, precious type of stone often carved to make jewellery and objects of art

junk—an ancient Chinese sailing ship

K, L

lacquerware—wood, cloth, or bamboo objects covered with many layers of varnish made from the sap of a tree

legacy—something of value inherited from someone no longer living

legend—stories from the past linked with real people and real events

M

magistrate—public officials in ancient China who enforced laws and judged court cases

martial arts—skills learned for fighting

merchant—a business person who buys and sells goods and produce; a trader

merit—to deserve a reward because of achievement or ability

metic—a resident of Athens who had not been born in Greece or a slave who had been freed

millet—a cereal grass with numerous small round grains in a head

monsoon—winds that change direction for winter and summer seasons

mythology—traditional stories about the gods and goddesses

N

natural resources—materials found in the environment that people use to meet their needs

naturalized—plants or animals introduced to a new place that have become part of the natural environment

O

oligarchy—a government where a small group of people has all of the power; oligarchs may be elected, appointed, or take power by force

oracle—a shrine with a priest or priestess believed to have the power to predict the future

oral tradition—stories of events and people of the past, passed on from adult to child and memorized

ostracize—(ancient Greece) to banish someone or send them away from the community for a period of time

P

peasants—poorer farmers who depended on the land to live rather than to make a profit; farm labourers or owners of small plots of land

peninsula—a piece of land surrounded on three sides by water, joined to a mainland by a narrow neck of land

phalanx—a square formation (arrangement) of Greek hoplites marching close together

philosopher—a person who thinks deeply about the physical world and human life

plateau—a high-elevation flat-topped landform

political life—the ways people organize and manage themselves and make decisions for the group; includes political structure, government and citizenship, the legal system, and defense and war

precipitation—moisture that falls as rain, snow, sleet, or hail (measured as rain)

public officials—people with government jobs who are involved in providing and managing government services

public works—projects managed by the government, paid for usually by taxes, for the benefit of everybody, such as roads and canals

Q

quarry—a place where pieces of stone are cut from the solid rock to be used for building material

quest—a long and difficult search for something special; often undertaken to prove one's courage and strength

R

rank—in ancient China, a person's level within the government service or the military

recorded history—events in the lives of people of the past that have been recorded in language or pictures

relief map—a map that shows the three-dimensional surface of the Earth

S

sacrifice—an offering, blessed and given to a god or goddess

sampan—a small flat-bottomed Chinese boat

scribe—a person who writes letters for customers or copies writing

scroll—in ancient China, a piece of silk or paper covered with calligraphy or painting that could be rolled up or hung

sediment—particles of earth and sand moved by a river

shrine—a special place dedicated to a god or goddess where people give offerings or prayers

slave—a person who was owned by and worked for another person, a business, or the government; in ancient Greece, slaves were most often prisoners of war or children of slaves

smelting—a process for removing metals from raw ore through high heat

social class—a set of people grouped together, as compared to other groups; a person's position in relation to others

social life—the ways people relate to each other and communicate; includes social structure, family, language, education, religion, arts, and sports/recreation

social structure—people in a group organized according to their roles, responsibilities, and rights

staple foods—foods that form the basic diet, usually eaten every day

state—an independent political unit with its own government, laws, and central administration

status—where a person stands in a social structure; high or low status may be based on birth, on wealth, or on merit

surplus—more of a product than is needed for daily life

T

technology—the tools and skills of a group of people

temple—a large public building used as a centre for religious activity

terraces—farm fields like stair steps on the side of a hill, used to increase the amount of agricultural land

terracotta—fired clay pottery or tiles, usually a reddish colour

trade—to exchange surplus products for other products that are needed or for money

tribute—an annual tax paid by a state to another state that conquered it

trireme—an ancient Greek warship rowed by three banks of oarsmen on each side, with a pointed bronze ram on the front for sinking enemy ships

U

unified—different parts made into a single whole

V, W

value—something that someone feels is important; something felt to have positive consequences

vendor—a person with something to sell

ward—sections or divisions of a city in ancient China

Index

A

Acropolis 46, 71, 73

agora 34, 36–38, 44–46, 71, 76. *See also* market

ancestors 118, 129, 141

ancient China 3, 80–146

ancient Greece 3, 6–77

animal life 4, 10, 16, 55, 90, 104, 113

apprentice 34, 37, 48

aquaculture 32, 90, 93

aqueduct 20, 29, 71

Archimedes 31

architecture 3, 6, 57, 62, 64, 96, 109, 135, 148

Aristotle 37, 50

armour 35, 65, 76, 130

army 26, 44, 73, 76, 77, 102, 103, 113, 117, 133, 134, 138, 141, 145, 146. *See also* military service

artifact 4, 5, 64

artisans 29, 34–38, 48, 55, 57, 109, 110, 117, 119, 131, 142

arts 3, 4, 6, 29, 52, 57–61, 64, 90, 97, 98, 107, 110, 113, 114, 121, 128, 131

astrology 118, 122

Athens 6, 9, 38, 39, 43, 46, 54, 57, 64–66, 70–74

athletics. *See* sports

B

Ban Zhao 124

basic needs. *See* needs

beliefs 42, 118, 128. *See also* religion

beverages 19, 93

birds 16, 46, 90, 104, 105, 119

bodies of water 4, 10, 12, 87, 88, 93

bronze 20, 22, 26, 32, 33, 35, 62, 65, 77, 97, 107, 109, 125, 131

Buddha 129, 131

builders 34, 43, 111

building materials 16, 22, 33, 64, 90, 96, 97

burial customs 3, 53, 55, 130, 139

business 29, 32, 34, 38, 44, 45, 97, 103, 111

C

calligraphy 121, 122, 131, 132

canals 31, 80, 93, 103, 105, 111, 117, 139

capital city 6, 9, 82, 83, 113, 124, 135, 140, 141

ceremonies 2, 3, 33, 53, 64, 109, 129, 131, 133

Chang Jiang (Yangzte River) 82, 87, 140

Chang'an 135, 140, 141

children 22, 24, 26, 29, 30, 42–46, 48, 65, 94, 97, 105, 118, 119, 122

cities 2, 3, 6, 8, 9, 15, 20, 29, 36, 38, 65, 70, 83, 103, 112, 140

citizen 37, 43, 44, 62, 72–74, 76

city-states 70–74, 76, 77

civilization 2–6, 80, 84, 86

class. *See* social class

clay 16, 20, 29, 35, 37, 90, 107, 130, 131

climate 4, 10, 14, 15, 24, 30, 31, 88, 89, 93, 104

clothing 4, 18, 24, 25, 34, 35, 45, 46, 92, 98, 99

colonies 8, 9, 39, 71, 83. *See also* settlements

communication 55, 103, 126, 139, 146. *See also* transportation, writing

communities 8, 32, 42, 43, 68, 70, 71, 86, 93, 141, 142

Confucius 122, 124, 125, 129

conscription 103, 145

cooking 20, 22, 45, 94, 95, 112, 119

craftspeople 29, 34–37, 43, 48, 103, 109–112, 140, 142

culture 4–6, 10, 42, 58, 70, 71, 86, 98, 117, 125

D

Daoism 125, 129

defense 4, 70, 76, 103, 113, 133, 140, 145, 146

democracy 3, 72, 73

deserts 82, 84, 86, 87, 113

dishes 20, 94, 109, 110

doctors 26, 36, 100, 103

dowry 44, 118

dynasty. *See* Han dynasty, Qin dynasty

E

economic life 4–6, 18–26, 28–40, 44, 92–100, 102–114

education 4, 29, 34, 37, 42, 44, 45, 48, 50, 116, 122, 124, 131, 140

elevation 14, 15, 86, 88

Emperor 109, 117, 126, 130, 132, 133, 138–141, 146

empire 102, 138, 139

entertainers 29, 43, 60, 109, 112

entertainment 44, 58, 60, 131, 133

environment 4–6, 8, 10–16, 18, 19, 22, 25, 28, 30, 32, 33, 40, 45, 70, 82, 84–90, 92, 100, 135

erosion 30, 64, 87, 104

export 19, 38, 39, 40, 71, 114

F

fabric 24, 25, 29, 35, 39, 40, 45, 46, 98, 99, 104, 112, 119

factories 29

families 4, 22, 24, 30, 32, 42, 44–46, 48, 97, 116–119, 122, 124, 125, 141–143

farming 16, 19, 25, 29, 30, 31, 36, 46, 54, 71, 86, 89, 97, 103–105, 112, 119

fertile land 16, 19, 30, 54, 56, 71, 82, 84, 86, 87, 90, 103

fish 16, 19, 20, 32, 90, 93, 94, 114

fishing 9, 11, 12, 19, 29, 32, 36, 87, 105

food 4, 18–20, 29, 30, 32, 36, 37, 56, 71, 77, 89, 90, 92–95, 100, 103, 112, 117, 143

forests 15, 89, 90

free men & women 29, 35, 37, 43, 72

furniture 23, 97, 109, 110, 131

G

games 45, 119, 136

gathering 16, 19, 104

gods and goddesses 20, 26, 33, 47, 48, 53–57, 59, 62, 64, 65, 76, 132. *See also* religion government 4, 6, 8, 29, 36, 43, 50, 68, 70–73, 102, 103, 109, 111, 117, 126, 138–143

government officials. *See* public officials

grain 19, 30, 40, 71, 89, 93, 97, 104, 113

Great Wall 82, 83, 139, 145, 146

gymnasium 22, 44

H

Han dynasty 82, 96, 122, 124, 126, 129, 132, 133, 135, 139, 140, 145

harmony with nature 96, 100, 125, 128, 129, 132, 135, 136

health care 4, 18, 26, 92, 100

herbalist 100, 103, 122

herbs 15, 19, 26, 92, 94, 100, 104

hereditary monarchy 72, 138, 141

hierarchy 117, 125, 141

Hippocrates 26

Homer 48, 58

homes 4, 18, 22, 23, 43–46, 53, 55, 62, 92, 96, 97, 109, 118, 119, 129, 135, 140

honey 16, 19, 30, 93

horses 48, 54, 57, 76, 113, 114, 134, 145, 146

Huang He (Yellow River) 82, 87

hunting 19, 55, 90, 104

I

import 19, 38–40, 47, 71, 102, 114

independent states 8, 70

industries 103, 109, 111

inventions 3, 31, 80, 105, 114, 125, 126

iron 11, 16, 26, 31, 33, 90, 98, 101, 103, 107, 111

iron smelting 107

irrigation 3, 12, 30, 31, 105

J

jade 90, 98, 107, 114, 130

jewellery 24, 33, 35, 90, 98, 107, 131

judge 73, 74. *See also* magistrate

junk 5, 114

K

kites 119, 120, 145

L

labourers 43, 103

lacquerware 94, 109, 110, 114

lamp 22, 97, 105

landforms 4, 10, 11, 82, 86

landowners 29, 30, 43, 103, 117, 135

language 2–4, 6, 8, 47, 70, 80, 121

Laozi 125, 129

latitude 14, 88

law 4, 36, 40, 43, 47, 54, 68, 70, 72–74, 139, 143

legacies iv, 19, 36, 40, 47, 50, 66, 70, 72, 74, 89, 95, 100, 110, 114, 126, 136, 148

legal systems. *See* law

libraries 58, 71, 124, 132

literature 47, 55–59, 131, 132, 148

M

magistrate 143. *See also* judge

marble 16, 33, 35, 40, 57, 62, 64

market 30, 34, 36, 37, 39, 46, 104, 112, 133. *See also* agora

marriage 43–46, 54, 118, 124, 143

martial arts 133, 136

mathematics 31, 38, 48, 50, 111, 125

meals 20, 94

meat 19, 53, 93, 94, 104

Mediterranean Sea 8, 9, 11, 39, 47, 71, 113

men 22, 24, 43, 58, 60, 65, 72, 94, 98, 103, 110, 116, 118

men's roles 26, 43–46, 48, 60, 119

merchants 29, 38–40, 43, 46, 111, 112, 117, 140

metals 16, 33, 35, 39, 40, 48, 90, 107, 109, 131

metics 43, 72

military service 26, 44, 65, 73, 76, 77, 134, 145

minerals 16, 90

mining 16, 29, 33, 39, 90, 107

money 29, 38, 44, 111, 126, 139

monsoon 88, 104

monuments 2, 3, 62, 139

Mount Olympus 11, 54

mountains 11, 12, 14, 15, 20, 33, 70, 82, 84, 86, 87, 113

Mulan (legend) 134

music 5, 48, 53, 59, 60, 77, 112, 122, 131, 133

musical instruments 35, 48, 54, 58–60, 77, 109, 112, 119, 133

mythology 54–56, 59, 99, 131, 132

N

natural resources 4, 10, 16, 90, 92

naturalized 89, 90

navy 26, 31, 39, 44, 77

needs 4, 10, 18–26, 28, 42, 44, 45, 52, 90, 92–100, 102, 109, 117

nobles 103, 117, 122, 139, 140

numbers 38, 111, 139

O

occupations 4, 28–40, 44, 98, 103, 141

olives 15, 16, 19, 20, 22, 30, 31, 39, 40, 54, 65

Olympic Games 65, 66

oracle 53

oral tradition 5, 48

ostracism 74

P

paper 40, 126, 131, 132, 148

Parthenon 57, 64, 71

peasants 103, 111, 117, 119. *See also* farming

performing arts 57, 60, 61, 133

Pericles 73

philosopher 37, 47, 48, 50, 57, 125, 131

plains 82, 84, 86, 87

plateaus 86

Plato 50

plays 47, 57, 60, 133

poetry 5, 47, 48, 57, 58, 124, 131, 132

political life 4–6, 36, 50, 68–77, 138–146

pomegranates 19, 56

pottery 16, 20, 29, 31, 34, 37, 39, 40, 57, 80, 94, 107, 109, 113, 131, 135

preserving food 32, 93, 107

priests & priestesses 43, 53

products 30, 36, 38–40, 71, 92, 100, 102–104, 111–114, 117, 126

protection 99, 109, 118, 129, 140

public buildings 4, 6, 34, 36, 53, 62
public officials 73, 103, 117, 124, 138, 141–143
public works 20, 29, 80, 103, 117, 138, 141
punishment 74, 103, 118, 143

Q
Qin dynasty 82, 130, 132, 139, 140
quarry 33, 90

R
religion 4, 20, 29, 43, 45, 52–56, 60, 64, 125, 128–131
responsibilities 43–46, 125, 129, 141, 143
rice 89, 93, 104, 105, 114
rights 29, 42–44
rivers 3, 12, 82, 87, 93, 105
roads 2–4, 29, 80, 103, 111, 117, 139, 146
roles 42–46, 116. *See also* men's roles, women's roles

S
salt 90, 93, 103, 104, 107, 111
sampan 105, 106
Sappho 58
scholars 117, 124, 132. *See also* teachers
school 37, 45, 48, 122, 142, 143. *See also* education
science 31, 47, 50, 111, 125, 132
sculpture 16, 33, 35, 57, 62, 64, 65, 107, 131
seas 8, 11, 12, 16, 32, 39, 47, 70, 87, 88, 107, 114
seasons 14, 30, 56, 87, 88, 89, 93
servants 29, 43, 96, 103, 135, 144
services 29, 102, 103, 112
settlements 8, 39, 47, 71
Shi Huangdi 130, 132, 139
ships 29, 38–40, 71, 77, 114
shrines 53, 64, 129, 131
silk 25, 40, 80, 98, 99, 103, 104, 109, 113, 114, 119, 126, 132, 136
Silk Road 113
silver 16, 33, 35, 39, 40, 98, 114

Skills
Creating a Map 69
Decision-making 63
Group Discussion 75
Making an Oral Presentation 108
Note-making 21
Reading Contour Lines 85
Reading for Information 13
Role-play 49
Writing a Biography 123
Writing a News Article 144
slaves 20, 22, 25, 29, 30, 33, 35, 37, 43–46, 59, 72, 74
social class 98, 99, 111, 116, 117, 131, 142
social life 4, 6, 42–50, 52–66
social structure 4, 42, 43, 116, 117, 124, 143
Socrates 50
soils 11, 15, 16, 19, 30, 87, 90
Sparta 65
sports 4, 44, 45, 48, 52, 65, 66, 128, 136, 148
sports facilities 22, 44, 65, 66
staple foods 20, 93, 95
state 70, 138, 139, 145
status 117, 118. *See also* social class
stone 16, 33, 90, 131. *See also* marble
story 11, 37, 46, 47, 58, 59, 124, 131, 132, 134, 136
symbols 99, 109, 118, 120, 125, 131, 135, 142, 143

T
taxes 70, 71, 76, 103, 111, 117, 138, 139, 141, 143
teachers 36, 45, 48, 50, 103
technology 2–4, 6, 20, 25, 26, 30–33, 48, 77, 80, 94, 104, 105, 107, 114, 125, 126, 145, 148
temples 26, 46, 53, 57, 62, 64, 71
terraces 30, 104
terracotta 29, 45. *See also* clay
terracotta warriors 130, 139
theatre 44, 60, 61, 71
thinkers 125, 132. *See also* philosopher, science, mathematics
tools 26, 31, 33–35, 104, 105, 107, 109, 117

toys 45, 119
trade 2, 4, 6, 8, 19, 25, 28, 29, 32, 38–40, 44, 47, 70, 71, 80, 90, 102, 104, 107, 111–114, 140
transportation 12, 30, 38, 40, 46, 71, 103, 111–113
trees 15, 19, 89, 110. *See also* forests
tribute 70, 71, 76
trireme 5, 77
tutor 45, 48, 123, 124. *See also* teachers
types of government 72, 138, 141

U
unified states 40, 70, 138, 139, 145

V
vegetation 4, 10, 11, 15, 16, 89, 90, 126
visual arts 5, 57, 131. *See also* sculpture
voting 43, 72, 73, 148

W
war 4, 26, 29, 31, 33, 43, 44, 54, 55, 57, 62, 64, 65, 70, 73, 76, 77, 113, 117, 130, 145
water 12, 14, 15, 19, 20, 45, 77, 87, 93, 113
weapons 35, 45, 76, 77, 107, 109, 113, 117, 130, 145
weaving 25, 29, 30, 34, 35, 45, 46, 109
wine 19, 20, 39, 40
women 22, 24, 25, 35, 43, 45, 46, 60, 65, 72, 74, 94, 98, 109, 118
women's roles 20, 25, 26, 29, 30, 43–46, 48, 60, 103, 119, 122, 124
work 28–38, 43, 44, 95, 102, 105, 107, 109, 111, 116, 119, 122, 131, 139
writing 2–4, 6, 26, 47, 48, 50, 57, 58, 80, 112, 120, 122, 124, 126, 132, 139

X, Y
yin-yang symbol 125, 129, 136

Ancient Greece

MACEDONIA

MT. OLYMPUS

THESSALY

Aegean Sea

Troy

LESBOS

PERSIAN EMPIRE

MT. PARNASSUS

Delphi

Gulf of Corinth

Thebes

Marathon

Corinth

Athens

Smyrna

Ephesus

Argos

Epidaurus

Miletus

Olympia

Halikarnassos

Jonian Sea

CYCLADES ISLANDS

Sparta

DODECANESE ISLANDS

⊙ City-State

Mediterranean Sea

0   100 KM

CRETE

Greece Today

10°W   50°N   0°   BELGIUM   10°E   POLAND   20°E   30°E   40°E

LUXEMBOURG   GERMANY   CZECH REPUBLIC   SLOVAKIA   UKRAINE   RUSSIA

FRANCE   AUSTRIA   HUNGARY   MOLDOVA

SWITZERLAND   SLOVENIA   ROMANIA   GEORG

40°N   CROATIA   YUGOSLAVIA   BULGARIA   Black Sea

PORTUGAL   SPAIN   ITALY   BOSNIA AND HERZEGOVINA   MACEDONIA   TURKEY

CORSICA   *Adriatic Sea*   ALBANIA

SARDINIA   *Jonian Sea*   GREECE   *Aegean Sea*   SYRIA

Mediterranean Sea   SICILY   Athens   CYPRUS

LEBANON   IRA

MOROCCO   ALGERIA   TUNISIA   CRETE   ISRAEL

30°N   JORDAN

0   500 KM   LIBYA   EGYPT   *Nile*   SAUDI ARABIA